If These WALLS *Could* TALK: PHILADELPHIA EAGLES

Stories from the Philadelphia Eagles Sideline, Locker Room, and Press Box

I0807716

Hugh Douglas with Mark Eckel

TRIUMPH BOOKS

Library of Congress Cataloging-in-Publication Data available upon request.

This book is available in quantity at special discounts for your group or organization. For further information, contact:

Triumph Books LLC
814 North Franklin Street
Chicago, Illinois 60610
(312) 337-0747
www.triumphbooks.com

Printed in U.S.A.
ISBN: 978-1-63727-980-9
Design by Patricia Frey
Page production by Nord Compo

To my son, Hugh Thomas,
there's not a day that goes by that you aren't thought about.
—Hugh Douglas

CONTENTS

FOREWORD

Hugh Douglas was both a teammate and a powerful presence. His edge, his humor, sometimes that loud and lovable irritation, it was all part of what made him essential and a respected leader.

In a league that depends on consistency, Hugh showed up every single practice and was an inspiration on game days. He brought energy when the room was flat and brought the heat when it was time to play.

He was always there. Reliable. Accountable. Always.

Mark Eckel is a hometown Trenton (N.J.) legend (the same city where I grew up). From day one there was mutual respect. Mark didn't just cover the Eagles, he cared. He was fair, even when he had to be critical. He told the whole story, not just the shiny side.

Through wins, losses, locker room highs, and heartbreak, Mark remained steady. A good writer. A trusted voice. A true sports journalist who painted reality with his words. He never forgot where he came from and told our stories with honesty and heart.

—Troy Vincent
Eagles Hall of Fame cornerback
current NFL executive vice president of football operations

AUTHOR'S NOTE

When Triumph, who I had written three books for previously, contacted me over a year ago and asked if I wanted to write a book with an Eagles player for the If These Wall Could Talk series, my first question was: Who's the player?

A quick reply said it was Hugh Douglas. It took less time than it did for Hugh to get to the quarterback for me to say yes. I had covered Hugh's entire career with the Eagles as both a beat writer and columnist for *The Trenton Times* and later nj.com. I actually broke the stories that he was going to sign with the Jacksonville Jaguars as a free agent, and, a little over a year later, that he was going to return to the Eagles. I also had the story first of his incident with Terrell Owens, which is told in detail in Chapter 16. Over my 32 years of covering the Eagles, Hugh was one of the players I enjoyed talking to and getting to know the most.

And talk, as the walls do, we did over the span of a few months. Over the following pages we try to bring you an inside look at the Eagles and some stories you may know, but with some details you may not know. And some other stories you probably never heard before. Hugh gives you his unique take from the locker room and what went on behind the scenes during his time with both the New York Jets and Eagles and even that one year in Jacksonville. And then later what he has observed as both a television and radio personality in Philadelphia and Atlanta. I do the same from my four different decades that included three owners, seven head coaches, a bunch of front office people, and God knows how many players in the press box for games and on the sidelines for practice.

What you see in regular Roman type like this is from Hugh. Anything in *italic like this* is my thoughts on the same subject. Here's hoping you enjoy what follows as much as Hugh and I enjoyed putting it together.

—*Mark Eckel*

CHAPTER 1
TRADED

I wanted to get traded. I asked to get traded. But I didn't want to go to Philly.

On March 13, 1998, a little over a month before the 1998 NFL Draft, the New York Jets traded defensive end Hugh Douglas to the Philadelphia Eagles for a second-round and a fifth-round pick in that upcoming draft.

I found out through Drew about the trade. Drew Rosenhaus, my agent, called me with the news. I had wanted to get out of New York. The Jets went to a 3-4 defense and I was frustrated. I had been Defensive Rookie of the Year (in 1995) and had like 10 sacks. Bill Parcells came in (as head coach in 1997) and we ran the same 4-3 defense all through training camp. They drafted (linebacker) James Farrior in the first round and we're playing the same 4-3 defense we played my first two years. Then right before the season starts—right before—we switch to a 3-4. Now, all of a sudden I become a defensive tackle at 260 pounds. Yes, a defensive tackle. I was playing in a 3-4 with a linebacker outside of me. I was basically playing a head-up technique, a 1-technique. And I'm getting manhandled. I'm frustrated. I'm not happy. We're winning, but I'm not happy. I want out. I don't like the way this is going—I don't like the way I'm being used—and I just want out. If I saw it coming, maybe it would have been different. Maybe I could have adapted. But it happened overnight, just like that. Looking back, they probably wanted to get Farrior, their first-round pick, on the field and more involved. I think that was it. And don't get me wrong, Farrior was a good player.

Farrior turned out to be a good pick and a good linebacker for the Jets. Douglas, however, went from a player with 18 sacks his first two years to just four in 1997. That immediate frustration didn't go away. It got worse.

I kept doing stuff to try to get cut or traded or whatever. I just wanted out. Drew said to just go in and tell them you want to be traded. So after the season I went to Bill Parcells and I told him, "I don't want to be here. I want to be traded." We had a conversation about it, but nothing happened.

Then all of a sudden one day I get a call from Drew and he says, "You've been traded. You got traded."

I was like, "Wow."

Somewhere along the line, Drew finally tells me I'm going to the Eagles. And I said, "I don't want to go to Philly." That was my initial thought: "I don't want to go to Philly. That's not where I want to go." I don't remember where exactly I wanted to go, or if there even was a specific place I wanted to go. But it wasn't Philly.

Several teams were interested and contacted the Jets about a potential trade. The Eagles, who were in desperate need of a pass rusher to play opposite their first-round pick from 1995, Mike Mamula, made the best offer, and the Jets didn't mind trading outside of the conference. Before the trade, however, Eagles president Joe Banner called former Eagles personnel employee Tom Gamble, who was with the Jets for Douglas' first two years and was now with the Carolina Panthers. "He wanted to know what kind of guy he was," Gamble said. "I told him to make the trade. That he was one of the few guys [with the Jets] who actually cared."

I really didn't know much about the Eagles. But I know I didn't want to go to Philly. I kept telling Rosenhaus that over and over. He called me back and said, "The trade has already been made. You're an Eagle.

I was like, "Shit." Then he said at this point they already traded for you so hell you can ask for anything you want. First thing I said is, "I want a new contract and I want number 53." That was the number I wore in college. I knew 99—my number with the Jets—was retired by the Eagles for Jerome Brown. I knew about Jerome, because our trainer with the Jets, David Price, used to work in Philly. He used to tell me stories about Jerome and how off the chart he was and how dominant he was. I knew I was not getting 99, so let me get my old number, my college number, 53.

Like I said, I really didn't know much about Philly or the Eagles. We played them in the preseason and it was in (Jackson) Mississippi. Yeah, we played them in Mississippi—so I hadn't even played in Philadelphia. When I say I didn't know anything about the Eagles, I *really* didn't. I mean, the guys I knew about, Reggie White, Jerome Brown, they were gone. I heard all the stories about Seth (Joyner) and how wild that team was. But they were all gone by the time I got there. I didn't know any of the guys on the current team.

Douglas and the Jets did play the Eagles late in the 1996 season at the Meadowlands and it took a 14-point fourth quarter for the playoff-bound Eagles to beat the one-win Jets, 21–20. Douglas had three sacks in the game and also recovered a fumble by Eagles quarterback Ty Detmer to help the Jets to a 20–7 lead going into that fourth quarter.

That game, yeah that was when Ty Detmer said something during the week like, "If we lose to the Jets we'll look like idiots." I was pissed. I was really pissed. I really wanted to win that game.

Two years later Douglas was on the other side of the Turnpike rivalry. Detmer was in San Francisco by then. However, his younger brother Koy was one of three Eagles quarterbacks on that 1998 team.

So I go in and I ask for the new contract and they say, "Fine. You want number 53? That's cool." They gave me the contract and they gave me the number and I became a Philadelphia Eagle.

A couple of days later I got to Philadelphia. We did the whole press conference thing. I remember right after that I found out they took number 53 from (defensive end) ND Kalu. They took his number and gave it to me. I didn't know that. I didn't know anyone had 53. And I felt bad about it. I'll never forget when I walked into the locker room for the first time. ND and (linebacker) Al Wallace were in there and they were sizing me up and down. And I'm sure they're looking at me and saying, "They traded for this little motherfucker." They were both bigger guys, bigger than me. And ND, I don't know if he said it, but I'm sure he's thinking, "They took my number and gave it to this motherfucker."

I walked up to him and said, "Hey man, I didn't know somebody had the number. Let me pay you for it. How does 10 grand sound?"

He said, "Cool." And that was that. We were good. I didn't need to come to a new team and come in and be an asshole. They took his number and I didn't know. So I made it right and I paid him for it.

I met (Eagles head coach) Ray Rhodes pretty early on, too. I told Ray what I wanted to do, and he told me what he projected me to do and a lot of other stuff. I remember Ray had a big dip (of tobacco) in his mouth and he was wearing an Eagles pullover. For me, I was just excited to have a Black head coach. He understood me. Playing for a Black head coach who spoke my language that was really cool. It was really starting to get familiar for me because I played for Billy Joe in college (at Central State), so it was cool to have Ray and then Emmitt (Thomas), a Black defensive coordinator. And (Mike) Trgovac, my defensive line coach, he was White, but he was Black, too (laughing). For me it was like being back at Central State.

You know what it was: Ray was relatable. Coming from the structure I had just come from under coach Parcells, it was just different. Coach Parcells came in and he didn't know us from Adam. He was trying to whip us into shape so to speak. I mean, we were coming off a one-win season. So he's trying to figure out—and I didn't realize it at the time—who he can depend on, who can play, who can he count on to do what he wants to do. And Ray that year, (quarterback) Bobby Hoying had played well at the end of the last year. They had been a playoff team (in 1995 and 1996). They needed someone on defense, they traded for me and they were glad to have me. Ray was a matter-of-fact kind of coach. He would tell stories in pregame. He had pregame speeches that were very, very descriptive. He would curse, he would curse a lot. And it resonated with a lot of people. Most of the coaches in the NFL then were White. He was one of the few Black head coaches in the league at that time.

Emmitt was quiet. He ran an intricate defense. But it was an all-inclusive defense. Everyone got a chance to talk. Everyone gave their feelings on how things should have been done. And what I liked was they just let me play. They let me get after the quarterback. And coming from what I just went through in New York, that's all I wanted to do.

I remember Emmitt saying, "Just let him go, because he's not wrapped too tight. Just let him play."

We played well defensively that year. We just didn't have an offense. But we loved Emmitt. We knew he was a great player (five-time Pro Bowl cornerback for the Kansas City Chiefs) and that mattered. It mattered to me. Hey, Parcells was a great coach. But he had a way of doing things that just didn't jibe well with me. The way I feel, most of the coaches today have success because they're relatable. I remember talking to (New York Jets head coach) Aaron Glenn when he was defensive coordinator for the Lions when they had all those injuries on defense (in 2024). He was getting guys off the street and they were playing hard for him because Aaron cared about those guys well-being. He had dinner with them and stuff like that. I was like, I never had a coach likes that except for Ray. He was a good coach. It's unfortunate the way it ended for him.

Rhodes first year with the Eagles he was the NFL Coach of the Year (I had a vote that year). He took a team that completely fell apart the year before, losing its last seven games, to a 10–6 record, a wild-card berth, and a blowout win over the Detroit Lions in the wild-card game. He made the playoffs the following year as well. Then it started to fall apart. The trade and a very good 1998 Draft that included five Pro Bowl players including Hugh Douglas, came too late. He was fired after a 3–13 season.

I met John Wooten early on too. He was the Eagles personnel guy at the time and I remember when I met him he told me they wanted to draft me, but they were a little afraid because I went to a small school. I guess they had a bad draft the year before and they didn't want to take a chance on me coming from a small school and all of that. At least that's what they told me.

Some players intend to play their whole career with the team that drafted them. It doesn't always work out that way. But it's usually their intention, especially when they win Rookie of the Year with a 10-sack rookie season and follow it up with an eight-sack, two-forced fumble, three-fumble recovery (one for a touchdown) second season. But that wasn't the case here.

To be honest, I never really liked New York. But I was there, so my thought was I'll play my four years and then I'll go where I go. I wasn't thinking past that. Remember, I'm not an East Coast guy or a big-city guy. I'm from a small town (Mansfield) in Ohio. I went to New York and there was some crazy shit going on there. I would go into the city and there were motherfuckers walking around naked. It was different. You would go down 42nd Street and see people dancing around naked. I wasn't used to that kind of stuff. Coming from that small town in Ohio, that wasn't me, not at all. I remember one of the first girls I met. She told me she just got out of rehab. Of course I think alcohol. She said, "No, cocaine."

I was like, "What the fuck? Cocaine. What!"

Now, Philly is a big city, too. But I have to say, Philly felt more like Ohio to me than it did New York. Now saying that, there are parts of Philly you can go to that have a New York feel. Old City, at that time, had the night life. But I could go to the suburbs and just chill. As a matter of fact when I first got there I actually lived in Cherry Hill (New Jersey). It was cool.

Getting to know his new teammates and forging what would become lifelong friendships made Philadelphia even more attractive. So on and off the field this was getting better and better.

I met Hollis (Thomas, the Eagles big defensive tackle) and some of the guys and I started to like it. Hollis was the first guy I really got to know. We had both come from small schools (Thomas came to the

Eagles from Northern Illinois as an undrafted rookie two years earlier), so we had that in common. I could relate to his plight. When you come from a small school you always have to prove yourself. It doesn't matter if you were a first-round pick or undrafted.

Hollis was over the top, though. I remember our first training camp at Lehigh (University) and Hollis was what they called my suite mate. Hollis brought a ton of Black adult magazines with him. And he says to me, "If you ever need any material, I got you." He was just funny as hell. But he helped me, too. He showed me the lay of the land and all of that. I got along with most of the guys right away, though.

You never know what's going to happen in professional sports. Players get released, traded, leave as a free agents. Sometimes it works out, sometimes it doesn't. This one worked out really well.

Listen, I learned a lot from Bill Parcells. I learned what it meant to be part of a unit. But in the moment, at twenty-something years old, I wasn't trying to hear none of that. I called Parcells (after the trade) and told him I didn't want to go to Philadelphia. He was at dinner at the time. He told me at that point it was out of his hands. We can't do anything about that now. They got you. Now just make the most of it. Years later he came to Philly—I'm not sure if he was still coaching the Jets, or maybe he was coaching the Cowboys—and I told him, "Thank You." He just smiled. I think he thought of me as a problem child. I think he thought I was uncoachable. And that year I would say, yeah, I was. I was undisciplined as a motherfucker. Because I just didn't give a fuck what they were trying to do. I was an individual at that point. I was playing for me.

What if the Jets stayed in their 4-3 scheme? Or what if instead of playing defensive tackle, the move was to outside linebacker? It's a question that will never be answered.

I don't think he thought I could play linebacker. Could I? If I had gotten the opportunity. I mean, I played stand-up pass rusher in college.

I don't know. He never even tried me at that position. I'm two-gapping in a two-gap system. So I started to freelance. I got a couple of sacks doing that. But I would get cussed out every day in the meetings, because I'm breaking down the technique of the defense.

The trade was good for me in a lot of ways. I did not fit what (the Jets) wanted. I just wanted to play football. I wanted to get after the quarterback. That's what I wanted to do, just play my game. So I needed to go somewhere else.

On the field, Philadelphia turned out to be the right place. There was a 12.5-sack season in 1998, the first year in Philly, followed by a 15-sack season in 2000 and a 9.5-sack season in 2001. That led to three straight Pro Bowls from 2000 to '02 and two years as an Associated Press All Pro (2000 and '02). That Eagles defense had three other Pro Bowl players in the secondary with Troy Vincent and Bobby Taylor at cornerback and Hall of Famer Brian Dawkins at safety.

Dawk wasn't Dawk yet. Not the Dawk he became anyway.

And off the field Philadelphia became home for the kid from the small town in Ohio.

I'm still here. I left for a little bit, but Philly became my home. Who knows what would have happened if I went somewhere else? If I got traded to San Francisco I might still be in the Bay Area. Andy Reid never becomes my coach. I may have never gone to a Super Bowl. Who knows? I may have never gone on radio. Because Derek Boyko (the Eagles public relations director at the time, now with the Buffalo Bills) is the one that got me to do radio in the first place. He told me I would be great on the radio. He pushed me into that. Everything would have been different. Going to Philly changed my life.

CHAPTER 2
DRAFT DAY

The Jets called and I almost said no. Really, I almost said no. They said, "Do you want to be a New York Jet?" and I almost said no.

With the 16th pick of the 1995 NFL Draft, the New York Jets selected Hugh Douglas, a defensive end out of Central (Ohio) State. Douglas didn't see it coming. He had met with the Jets, but others teams had shown more interest right up until he got the call.

I had talked to Larry Lee, who was a big part of the Detroit Lions (as vice president of football operations) and Robert Porcher (Detroit's first-round pick in 1992), who went to South Carolina State. I kind had a good rapport with (Porcher). When I went to visit the Lions I met Porcher and it went really well. Seeing him doing well, coming from a small school like South Carolina State, it gave me a reason to think I could do the same. I honestly thought I might be a Detroit Lion. So I'm sitting at home and as they're getting ready to call my name I'm on the phone with the Lions. For all intents and purposes they were going to take me. (The Lions had the 20th pick of the first round). Then the Jets called. And like I said, I almost said no. Then I thought, "You went to a small school, you came out of nowhere, and you're getting drafted. If you don't fucking say yes …." So I said yes. But I was really going to say no.

Douglas was not at the draft in New York where a lot of the top picks gather to hear then-commissioner Paul Tagliabue call their names. He was with his agent in Dayton, Ohio, a couple hours away from his home in Mansfield.

I was with Ron Todd and associates then. Coming from a small school and all of that, nobody knew if I was going to get drafted. It was more like, "Wow." I was Hugh from the neighborhood. "Oh that motherfucker about to get drafted? Wow." So nobody was there, because nobody knew. My family was in Mansfield. My people are old school. They weren't going to travel. Nobody is coming to Dayton from Mansfield because I might get drafted. It wasn't a guarantee.

I was told early on that's why I wasn't going to be invited to the draft, "Because we don't want you to be embarrassed if you're not drafted." So

I didn't go. I went 16th, but nobody expected that. Yeah, I did well at the Combine, but at the end of the day nobody knew. I was still a kid from a small school.

Scouts and personnel people always say if you're from a small school, you had better be dominant at the small school to make it in the NFL. Douglas was just that. In three years at Central (Ohio) State, he had 42 sacks in 32 games and was a two-time NAIA first-team All-American. While being from a small school scared off some teams (the Eagles actually told Douglas after they traded for him three years later that was one of the reason they passed on him), there were a few teams, such as the Lions, Steelers, and obviously the Jets, who were not afraid to take a chance on a small-school standout.

Dick Haley and Todd Haley (the Jets general manager and his son), we had conversations. But I didn't think I was going to get drafted by the Jets, I really didn't. They had two picks, but I didn't think I was going to be one of their picks. The Eagles told me they thought about it, but didn't pull the trigger. The Eagles said they wanted to draft me, but at the end of the day it was the small-school thing. They were afraid to make a first-round pick on a kid from a small school. They didn't want to take that chance. I visited Minnesota. I was a big fan of (All-Pro defensive lineman) John Randle, got a chance to see them practice, and liked it. Pittsburgh was another team. I met with (head coach) Bill Cowher. He said, "How would you like to be a Steeler?"

I said, "Coach, I want to play." They had Kevin Greene and Greg Lloyd at the time. I wanted to play. With those guys there, there's not a whole lot of playing going on for me. I would have loved Pittsburgh, but how was that going to go?

I think my (Scouting) Combine helped me. I did a combine workout every day to get ready. I stayed with Ron Todd and Martin Bayless' mother. (Bayless, another Ohio native, was a fourth-round pick of the Cardinals out of Bowling Green in the 1984 Draft). She took care of me. She was the one who made sure I got my meals every day and really went out of her way for me. I just stayed with them and worked out from the time I left school until the Combine started. Gerald (Bayless, a tight end from Bowling Green) was big in the community of Dayton, still is, and he was the guy who made it happen. The Bayless family took me in and got me ready for the combine and the NFL.

All the prep work paid off. Douglas did well in Indianapolis. At 261 pounds, he ran a 4.76 in the 40, had a 32-inch vertical, a 113 in the broad jump, and did 27 reps of 225 pounds in the bench press. It was enough to get picked 16th overall. The Eagles, like many teams, were enamored with and fell in love with another defensive end, Mike Mamula, from Boston College, who had an incredible performance at the same Combine. He ran a 4.62 in the 40, had a 38-inch vertical, and 123 in the broad jump.

I remember I'm talking to the Chicago Bears (in an interview at the Combine) and all of a sudden everyone is talking about this dude from Boston College who just blew up the Combine. Oh shit, he killed it. I was like, "Who is this guy?" and of course it was Mike Mamula. It was one of those things, Mike had one of the all-time Combines.

It didn't hurt that Eagles owner Jeffrey Lurie, who had bought the team a year earlier, was a Boston native when the team traded up from the 12th pick to the seventh pick with the Tampa Bay Buccaneers to select Mamula. Tampa Bay dropped to 12th and selected future Hall of Famer Warren Sapp. As irony would have it, Douglas and Mamula became teammates and linemates three years later after the trade to the Eagles. They played together for two years with Douglas at right defensive end and Mamula on the left side.

Mike was a good dude. If you think about it, Mike was put in a bad spot. He went to a big school, had a hell of a combine, like we said, and they drafted him early. He was on the cover of *Sports Illustrated.* He was that dude. And now he's going to a place and a team where they were looking for someone to be that dude. Reggie White was gone. Jerome (Brown) was gone. They were looking for that next guy. And he was going to be it. So you know Mike was picked to be that dude. He was a good player, but he wasn't that. He wasn't what Philly wanted or needed. Philadelphia is a difficult place. There are certain guys the city just loves, like Andy Harmon. Big dude, got after the quarterback, they loved that cat. They didn't love Mike.

This is how the draft went up until the Jets were on the clock at No. 16 and Douglas was on the phone with the Lions.

Cincinnati: Ki-Jana Carter, RB, Penn State

Jacksonville: Tony Boselli, T, Southern Cal

Houston: Steve McNair, QB, Alcorn St.

Washington: Michael Westbrook, WR, Colorado

Carolina: Kerry Collins, QB, Penn St.

St. Louis: Kevin Carter, DE, Florida

Philadelphia: Mike Mamula, DE, Boston College

Seattle: Joey Galloway, WR, Ohio St.

Jets: Kyle Brady, TE, Penn St.

San Francisco: J.J. Stokes, WR, UCLA

Minnesota: Derrick Alexander, DE, Florida St.

Tampa Bay: Warren Sapp, DT, Miami

New Orleans: Mark Fields, LB, Washington

Buffalo: Ruben Brown, OL, Pitt

Indianapolis: Ellis Johnson, DT, Florida

The Jets made Douglas the fourth defensive end selected after Carter, Mamula, and Alexander. Only Carter, with 104 sacks in 14 seasons and two Pro Bowl selections, came close to Douglas' 80 sacks in 10 years and three Pro Bowl selections.

Rich Kotite, fired by the Eagles after the team lost its last seven games of the 1994 season to go from 7–2 to 7–9 in the greatest collapse in NFL history, was named the Jets head coach before the 1995 Draft. Already armed with the ninth overall pick of the draft the Jets acquired the 16th pick in a trade with the Arizona Cardinals for wide receiver Rob Moore. They used that acquired pick on the small-school defensive end.

I was a first-round draft choice but people still looked at me like I didn't belong. I remember that. I remember the first day of training camp with the Jets. We're not in pads yet and I forget who the guy was but this dude jacked me up at practice. I got pissed. I was like, "Okay, they don't respect me. I'm going to make them respect me." I got in a fight nearly every day. I got into with (Pro Bowl tackle) Jumbo Elliott one day. We doing one-on-ones and he threw me down. Marvin Washington says to me, "Oh you just going to let him do you like that. You're going to let him manhandle you like that."

The next one on one I ran into Jumbo and slammed him to the ground and started swinging on him, hitting him. He got up and I thought Jumbo was going to beat the shit out of me. Marvin jumped on top of Jumbo and I remember Jumbo said, "Marvin, if you don't get off me I'm going to fuckin' kill you." Now I go back into the locker room and I'm thinking Jumbo is going to kill me. I mean Jumbo is a big man. I'm at my locker and I'm waiting for Jumbo to come by. I got my hand on my chair, because I'm thinking if he comes at me, I'm going to hit him with this chair. He let it go. He walked past me and just kept going. He just left me alone.

While Douglas was the Jets first-round pick, he wasn't their first overall pick. As the chart above shows, they took Penn State tight end Kyle Brady ninth overall. Brady played 13 years in the league. He left the Jets after four years, one year after Douglas, and spent the next eight years with the Jacksonville Jaguars. His final season was with the New England Patriots. He had a decent career, but one not worthy of being the ninth overall pick.

Kyle was cool. He never said a lot. He just wanted to play. He just wanted to be the tight end. He was coming from Penn State and they had a great year. I think it was their first year in the Big 10 and they ran roughshod. They had three guys drafted in the top 10, Ki-Jana Carter, the quarterback Kerry Collins, and Kyle. They were bona fide.

While Penn State had three players go in the first round in 1995, Douglas was just the sixth player ever drafted out of Central State (Mel Lunsford, third round, 1972, Oakland; Curtis Anderson, fifth round,1979, Dallas; Vince

Buck, second round, 1990, New Orleans; Erik Williams, third round 1991, Dallas; and Roosevelt Nix, 1992, eighth round, Cincinnati). Four more have been drafted since and he is still the only one to be selected in the first round.

Buck, a defensive back, spent six years in the league, all with the Saints. He started four of his six years and finished his career with 10 interceptions and 12 fumble recoveries.

Williams played 11 years in the league, all but one with the Cowboys, and became known as one of the best right tackles in the game. The Philadelphia native was named to four Pro Bowls.

Big E (Erik Williams) was in a league of his own. He was a Philly guy. He really wanted to get drafted by the Eagles and was mad they didn't take him. He made them pay every time he played against them.

It was a big deal getting drafted from Central. My coaches kept telling me I was going to get drafted. And they were the ones who talked to the scouts. I didn't know what was going to happen. I really didn't. I didn't want to put all my eggs in that one basket. All I knew is all these White folks, scouts and personnel guys, are up here talking to me every day from different teams. I was just going to take it as it comes. I'm not going to get too high or too low. I didn't want to be disappointed. What if I didn't get drafted? So if it happens, it happens. That was my attitude the whole time.

It happened and it happened pretty early. Being the 16th overall pick isn't an accident. And if the Jets didn't take him at 16, it appeared the Lions were going to do so at No. 20. They ended up with a pretty good player in defensive tackle Luther Elliss, instead.

Yeah, but to be honest, at that point (being picked 16th) now there's work to be done. To be picked that high there's all kinds of expectations. And I felt that heat before the first preseason game. Cats are looking at me and still saying, "He's not supposed to be here. Did we draft the right guy?" After the Draft, I get to New York and I remember this like it was yesterday, these people are looking at me like, "Who the fuck is this guy? Who is this from this small-ass school trying to play at this level?"

I had a chip on my shoulder. I've always had a chip on my shoulder. I would see it, and hear it. Guys would say, "Where is Central State? I never heard of Central State."

I was like, "Motherfucker, it's in Ohio." We got guys from Southern Cal and Penn State and Notre Dame. They would all look down on me. And I would internalize everything. I would tell cats, "I'll just beat your ass." I definitely had an attitude.

Despite all of that and almost saying no to the Jets, it didn't take long for Hugh to sign his first NFL contract and to spend some of that first signing bonus.

I signed pretty fast. My agent was kind of new to the game. So it didn't take long for me to sign. And then I was living high on the hog. You know how they say that? Well I was living high on the hog. First thing I bought was a 1995 Black Chevy Impala SS. I was always a Chevy guy and that was the new hot Chevy that was out that year. So I went out and bought one.

Douglas' draft day was interesting to say the least: Almost telling the team that drafted him he didn't want to play for them; getting picked earlier than anyone, including himself and his family, expected; and if he had his way he wouldn't have even been around to hear his name called.

If I'm not mistaken, the draft was on a Friday my year. And I wanted to go to Black College Weekend in Atlanta. I kept telling my agent I wanted to go to Atlanta. I didn't want to stick around for the draft. I figured the draft is what it is. I want to go to Atlanta. My agent was like, "Hugh, you have to be in town. If a team calls and you're not here that's not a good look. You have to be here." I didn't care. I wanted to go to the Freaknik. I wanted to meet people. But he was right, so I stayed for the draft.

And then ...

As soon as it was over and I was drafted I headed straight to Atlanta.

CHAPTER 3

ROOKIE OF THE YEAR

I just wanted to work hard and break that stereotype of, "You're from a small school you can't play at this level." And I remember after just the second game of the season, I didn't have a sack and people started looking at me sideways. It was only the second game of the season and it was like, "Did we draft the wrong guy?" There were a couple stories that alluded to that. They were setting it up on me. It was crazy.

In his third game, Douglas recorded three sacks against the Jacksonville Jaguars on his way to a 10-sack rookie season that earned him the NFL's Defensive Rookie of the Year Award. The voting wasn't even close. Douglas received 57 of the 88 votes cast to easily outdistance Minnesota Vikings safety Orlando Thomas, who finished second with 25 votes. Two of Douglas' future teammates with the Eagles, cornerback Bobby Taylor and defensive end Mike Mamula, finished third and fifth respectively.

At the time (winning the award), it made me feel great, but the funny thing was winning Rookie of the Year and being in New York it was kind of like, that's nice, but we weren't good. We weren't good at all. Being the Rookie of the Year, I appreciate it more now that I'm older then I did when it happened. I was playing for the Jets, and it was a time when, what people remembered about the Jets was the New York Sack Exchange and Mark Gastineau and all of those guys. So I win Rookie of the Year and people are like, "That's great, but you play for the Jets." So it wasn't that big of a deal. Playing for the Jets wasn't like playing for the Eagles or the Giants. It was the Jets. The fan base were a lot of long suffering Jets fans. So to be honest I really never thought about it until you brought it up that it was a big deal.

It was a big deal for a kid from Central (Ohio) State, who wasn't sure he was going to be drafted, to becoming the 16th overall pick to winning the award over the other four defensive linemen chosen ahead of him and a few chosen after him. All of them also being from Power conferences in college and playing for better teams than the 3–13 Jets.

Now that I think about it that was pretty impressive (winning the award for a three-win team). At the time, nobody really cared about it, it was like, you won Rookie of the Year, big deal.

Douglas' 10 sacks led all rookies, as did his two fumble recoveries. Kevin Carter, the first defensive end selected (sixth by the Rams) had six sacks. Mamula, selected seventh by the Eagles, had 5½. Derrick Alexander, selected 11th by the Vikings, had two. Future Hall of Famer Warren Sapp, taken 12th by the Tampa Bay Bucs, only had three his rookie season. Mamula and Taylor, the Eagles first two selections in that 1995 Draft, helped the team erase that seven-game losing streak that ended the 1994 season and to a 10–6 1995 season that earned them a NFC wild-card berth and rookie head coach Ray Rhodes the NFL's Coach of the Year Award.

Bobby (Taylor) balled out. They drafted him because he was tall to cover (Dallas') Michael Irvin and he did. They wanted a tall corner, because Michael was tall. To me Bobby was really underrated, for real. He was an underrated corner. Bobby was a hell of a player. And Bobby still looks like he could play. We were in New Orleans, me, Takeo Spikes, and Bobby were together. I said, "Bobby, out of all these cats who played football you're the only one who looks like you still can. The rest of us, no."

I did (watch the other rookies) a little bit. I watched Derrick Alexander. Because I remembered him vividly and he didn't do that well his rookie year in Minnesota. Kevin Carter did well. I don't think he had as many sacks his first year, but he had a good career. Kevin was your prototypical defensive end through and through. He was the guy who could play inside and outside. He was one of those bigger dudes with those long arms. I had to play more physical because of my size. My game was physical as far as my pass rush. It had to be.

Douglas entered the league at 6'1", 265 pounds. In today's NFL the 6'1" might still be considered short, but the 265 is a good-sized defensive end. For instance, of the top eight defensive ends selected in the 2025 NFL Draft, only three were bigger than 265.

I was considered small. I came in at the end of an era where most defensive linemen were 6'5", 6'6", and long. Now it's gone to smaller guys, who are quicker. I would have been big in the draft now.

Douglas' NFL debut was about as tough of an assignment as a rookie could imagine. It was against the Miami Dolphins in Miami. The team that would earn an AFC wild-card berth that year beat the Jets, 52–14, behind three touchdown passes from Hall of Fame quarterback Dan Marino. Ironically, two future Eagles and one former Eagle scored touchdowns in the game for the Dolphins. Wide receiver Irving Fryar caught two of Marino's three touchdown passes and cornerback Troy Vincent, who wrote the foreword for this book, returned an interception 69 yards for a touchdown. Fullback Keith Byars, the Eagles first-round pick in 1985, caught Marino's third touchdown pass.

It's my first game in the NFL and we played against the Dolphins and Dan Marino. The first thing was we were in Miami and we got blown out. Next, I remember Keith Byars. I remember him catching a crossing route and he took it to the house. I'm looking at him and I'm saying to myself, "How does his big ass move that fast with those little feet." He barely looks like he's running. I'm saying, "Wow." And I know him because he's from Ohio and went to Ohio State. And it was like, "Damn. Look at him." And they're just putting it on us. They beat the shit out of us.

Now for me, I'm going against (left tackle) Richmond Webb. I'm trying to get to Dan Marino. I always say I had the best seat in the house to watch Dan Marino play. Because I damn sure didn't touch him. You're talking about a Hall of Fame (finalist) tackle in Richmond Webb. Nobody could be mad at me that day for not getting a sack. But the next week the motherfuckers are saying, "I'm not sure the Jets took the right dude."

It's Richmond Webb! And it's Dan Marino. He got the ball out of his hand so damn fast. He was like a conductor. I remember that game like it was yesterday. They went no huddle. He's telling people where to go and you run this route and you run that route. And I'm standing there watching. Remember it's my first game, and I'm like, "He's good. Wow, he's really good at what he does."

Two weeks later, Douglas was really good in the first of the Jets three wins that season, a 27–10 thumping of the expansion Jacksonville Jaguars. The Jaguars would finish their first season, 4–12, one game better than the Jets. In Week 3, however, it was the Jets and Douglas who had their way.

What happened was (Hall of Fame left tackle) Tony Boselli was Jacksonville's first-round pick, but he got hurt. He was hurt that game. So they had a backup tackle. And I worked that cat like a shift. And after that it kind of all fell into place for me. The game started to slow down for me.

After the three-sack performance in the win over Jacksonville, Douglas had sacks in three consecutive games against the Atlanta Falcons, Oakland Raiders, and Buffalo Bills. The Jets lost all three games by double figures. The Raiders game was another blowout as Oakland rolled, 47–10. So while the Jets dropped to 1–5, their first-round draft pick was more than showing he belonged.

When we played the Bills I remember watching Bruce Smith. Now I didn't have the body type of Bruce Smith. But I remember Bruce got off the ball, I mean he really got off the rock. And he was a little older at that point (32). And that whole Buffalo defense was really good. They also had (rush linebacker) Bryce Paup (who was the NFL's Defensive Player of the Year in 1995 with17½ sacks) and (nose tackle) Ted Washington. But I watched Bruce Smith line up at his end spot. And as I watched him I remembered reading about him and how he worked out all the time. Be on the treadmill, be on the StairMaster, all that cardio he did. So let me get my ass doing cardio. I started to think I might not be as big as Bruce Smith, but nobody is going to outwork me. That's where it all came from, watching guys like Bruce and Reggie White. Knowing I did not have the kind of size they had, but nobody is going to work harder than me. If you're out there (against me) you're going to know I put homework in, because I'm going to put it on your ass. I was almost always at a size disadvantage. I was always at a height disadvantage. So if I do lose, you're going to know you were in for a long day. You had a long-ass day.

That hard work was instilled in Douglas from his days at Central State playing for legendary coach Billy Joe. One of the greatest small college coaches ever, Joe played his college ball at Villanova, played in the AFL for seven years, won a Super Bowl with the Jets in 1969, and was a college assistant for years. He became the Eagles running back coach in 1979 and was there in 1980 for the team's first trip to the Super Bowl. He was the head coach at Central State from 1981 to 1993, where he compiled an incredible record of 120–30–4.

Coach Joe was a scary dude, but he was smart. We had this thing called "Pirate Night." Where you're not a Marauder (Central's nickname), you're a Pirate. They initiate all the freshmen. One time it went south and Coach Joe found out and he was a on a tear. "I told you to leave these kids alone." He was different. He could be a monster, but he knew football. One thing about Coach Joe I'll always remember is he used to always tell us never let the guy behind you show what he can do. I'll tell you what, that's something I live by to this day. Like when they talk about going on vacation at work, "No, I'm cool." Because it happened to him. I forget the running back's name, but when (Joe) was with the Jets he got hurt and this guy took his job. Then, he got traded. He was like, "They got my ass out of there." But he was a really, really good coach.

There's another memory from Central State that Douglas never forgot either.

I remember one time at Central just before the draft, I inadvertently walked into the room where a scout was watching film on me. It was a Green Bay scout. I don't know his name, but he was from Green Bay because he was wearing a Packers polo shirt. He said, "You're Hugh Douglas. Man, you play hard on every play. Don't ever lose that." He was honest. He told me the competition I'm playing against isn't that great, "But the fact that you're relentless, you have a shot. Don't ever lose that, don't lose that motor."

He never did. And he relays that message now to other small-school players dreaming that NFL dream.

I went to Delaware State to watch (former Eagles wide receiver) DeSean Jackson coach and I told the guys, "Listen, you're going to a small school. I went to a small school. You have some good coaches here who played in the NFL, just like I did. Now I'm going to be honest with you, you might not make it to the NFL but you got a chance if you play hard. Because if you play hard they'll find you. Because they found me. I went to a D-II school in Wilberforce, Ohio. So play hard and listen to what's being taught, and you will have a shot. And really that's all you can ask. Going to Central State there were a couple of guys who went (to the NFL) before me. But I always had what I like to call "the little-man complex." And that was exaggerated by the fact that when I went to New York cats were like, "We really drafted this guy with a first-round pick?"

CHAPTER 4
RICH KOTITE AND 4–28

I remember talking to Rich Kotite about us losing and how I'm getting kind of tired of it. And he said, "Don't worry, babe, it will get better." But it never did.

No it didn't. Not for the New York Jets or head coach Rich Kotite. Kotite coached the Eagles for four years (1991–94). He and Douglas arrived in New York in 1995. The team went 3–13 that first year and 1–15 in 1996. Of course, Kotite was fired.

He'd also been fired—or, to be fair, had not had his contract renewed—in Philadelphia after the 1994 season, when his team completed what is still the greatest collapse in NFL history. After a 7–2 start to the season, the team lost its last seven games to finish 7–9. No other NFL team has ever started a season 7–2 and not finished at least .500. Ironically, when the team was 7–2 and Kotite was in the final year of his contract he was asked about his job status. "I think my record speaks for itself," he told the Philadelphia Inquirer. *His record from that time on with the Eagles and the Jets was 4–35. And he never coached again, even on the assistant level.*

I liked Coach Kotite, because, well, he drafted me.

It was one of the few good decisions he made in his two years with the Jets. Or for that matter in his four years with the Eagles. Kotite, who was the Jets receivers coach, was hired by the Eagles before the 1990 season as offensive coordinator under Buddy Ryan to replace Ted Plumb, who had been fired by Ryan a few weeks prior. He was recommended to Ryan by Eagles president Harry Gamble, and then, when Hall of Fame quarterback Joe Namath also called Ryan with an endorsement, the deal was done. Ryan was the Jets defensive coordinator when Namath came through with his guarantee to win Super Bowl III and there had been mutual admiration ever since.

When Ryan was fired after the Eagles lost in the first round of the playoffs in 1990, Kotite thought he was gone as well. He's recently told people he was on the phone with his wife telling her he would be looking for a job. That job became head coach of the Eagles when owner Norman Braman chose him over defensive coordinator Jeff Fisher. In one of the quickest coaching decisions ever made, Ryan was fired the morning of January 8, 1991, and Kotite was hired later that afternoon. I remember vividly writing the story of Ryan's firing, along with another story with the player's perspective and a list of prospective replacement. Former University of Miami head coach Howard Schnellenberger was near the top of that list. As I was ready to leave the Eagles' workroom at old Veterans Stadium and go home, the team's public relations man Ron Howard said to me, "You might want to stick around." Uh oh.

What I remember is Coach Kotite being out there on the practice field with that big-ass cigar. And he had this guy, Matty (McIntyre, his longtime friend from Staten Island), his guy with him all the time. That was his guy. We didn't know who he was, but he was Coach's guy. They were always together.

The Jets quarterback in 1995 was Boomer Esiason, who had taken the Cincinnati Bengals to the Super Bowl in 1988 and back to the playoffs in 1990. This was his third season with the Jets and they all ended short of the playoffs.

Boomer thought he was the quarterback and everyone else was beneath him. He was old guard. He went to a Super Bowl so he thought he was better than the rest of us. And he was pissed off when they got rid of him (after the 1995 season). Then he went to Arizona and did pretty well. He played well in Arizona.

As far as the rest of the team, (Kotite) brought in a veteran group for the most part. He brought in Matt Brock from Green Bay. He had Marc Spindler, Marvin Washington, Erik Howard, we had a bunch of older guys who had been in the league. But he had Reggie (White), Jerome (Brown), Clyde (Simmons), Seth (Joyner), and all of those guys in Philly. These guys weren't those guys.

In practice, we would fuck up a play and he would never correct it. He would say, "It's okay. We'll get it tomorrow, babe."

I remember even as a rookie saying, "What?" I had never been around something like that before. When you fuck up something you got cussed out for it. And as far as tomorrow went, we usually fucked it up again.

Eagles fans tried to warn Jets fans what they getting, but they didn't want to listen. There was excitement on Long Island where the team practiced and was headquartered. Kotite was the guy to take the Jets back to the playoffs and just maybe the Super Bowl. Going 4–28 wasn't in the plans. And Eagles fans were all too happy to say, "Told ya so." For Douglas, the losing was painful and an unknown. At Central State he went to two NAIA National Title games, winning one and losing one. Now, he was 4–28 in his two seasons in the NFL.

It was tough. But believe it or not, being in New York, it wasn't as bad as you might think. You were the story for like a day. There were so many other teams and sports in New York that the Jets losing was a story for a day, one day. And then they moved on to something else. And I might be wrong, but people kept coming to the games. There were a bunch of Jets fans out there every Sunday. The difference with Jets fans is they don't wear their fandom like Eagles fans do. It was more, you are disappointed on Sunday, then you get over it. And they would be back there the next Sunday, or the next home game. Eagles fans are mad all week, sometimes even when we won. For me the biggest thing being in New York was I felt out of place. The losing was bad, for sure, but it was more so being a kid from a small town in a big city. I stayed at home for the most part. I didn't really go anywhere.

Neither did the Jets. After the embarrassing three-win 1995 season that saw the Jets rank 30th (of 30 teams) on offense and 26th on defense, they ranked 27th and 29th respectively in 1996 when the record dropped to 1–15. The season started as bad as you would expect with two losses to two playoff-bound teams, a 31–6 loss at Denver and a 21–7 loss at home to Indianapolis. In Week 3 at Miami, injury replaced insult when Douglas suffered a broken ankle in a loss to the Dolphins.

(Miami running back) Stanley Pritchett rolled up on me. He rolled on my ankle and I heard it break. It was like *cruuuunch* and I was like "Ahhhhhh!" I was yelling like a bitch. It was the first time I really got hurt playing. I broke my hand once before, but that wasn't that bad. I didn't miss any time or anything.

It was hard. I'm wearing a cast. I'm walking with crutches. But the worst part was we're losing, I'm not playing and I'm by myself in New York. I really didn't know anybody, so I kind of just stayed to myself. Actually, I was afraid of New York. It was different in New York, especially for me being from a small town. They were into some different shit. It was really different.

When I got hurt they said it would be about six weeks before the bone would heal. But something funny happened with the way the bone healed and I was able to play sooner than they first thought.

Douglas missed six games with the broken ankle, including the Jets only win, a 31–21 decision over the Arizona Cardinals. The following week was the bye. And Douglas returned the next week against the New England Patriots. Boy, did he return. He had a sack in that first game back against the Pats and then two against the Colts and quarterback Jim Harbaugh the following week.

My ankle was still on fire, but I wanted to play. I had to wear an ankle support because where it was broken was still kind of soft. It hurt like a mother.

So did the losing. And it got personal when the Jets, at 1–13, were getting ready to host the 8–6 Eagles, who were battling both for first place in the NFC East with the Dallas Cowboys and for one of the three wild-card berths with the Washington Redskins and Minnesota Vikings. The Eagles, as they did in Kotite's final season two years earlier, began the season 7–2. And almost in the same fashion began to crumble. They headed to the Meadowlands to play the Jets losers of four of their past five games. It was about as much of a must-win game as there was. The Wednesday before the game Eagles quarterback Ty

Detmer was asked about the game and the importance of it. He said among other things, "If we lose to the Jets we look like idiots."

Somebody told me about it, one of the (Jets) writers. I said something to the effect of I'm going to do something to hurt him or some shit like that. I said some real wild shit. It was bad enough we're losing every week, but to hear stuff like that, I just went off. Then I got a letter from the league that said if something were to happen to (Detmer) during the course of the game you will be fined. I was like, "Oh wow." I didn't realize what I said. I was just pissed at what he said. I wasn't about to get fined over this. So I just went out and played. I wanted to be a one-man gang. I wanted to beat the fuck out of the Eagles that day. And we lost by one point. I mean we were getting our ass kicked every week. So (Detmer) actually had a good point. But sometimes you don't like to hear the truth.

The Jets led 20–7 going into the fourth quarter. Quarterback Glenn Foley connected with Keyshawn Johnson on a 46-yard touchdown pass. Nick Lowery added two short field goals and Detmer kind of looked like "an idiot" when Jets cornerback Aaron Glenn (now their head coach) returned an interception 13 yards for a touchdown. And Douglas was killing the Eagles 1996 first-round pick Jermane Mayberry, who started at tackle that day in place of an injured Barrett Brooks. Mayberry, who would later become a Pro Bowl guard, played tackle that day and was abused by the fired-up Douglas who was relentless all day. Douglas recorded the second three-sack game of his young career and also forced a Detmer fumbled.

Oh, I was talking. I don't know if anyone was talking back, but I was talking. I talked shit that whole day. I really wanted to win that game. I was talking so much I think Ray (Rhodes) actually liked it. And Emmitt (Thomas) was like, "That guy is crazy." I know I was yelling and screaming at people, yelling at their sideline. I was running my mouth so much they had to be thinking, "There's something wrong with him." I think that may have had something to do with them trading for me.

The Eagles won their final game of the season against the Arizona Cardinals to finish 10–6 and tie with Dallas for first place in the East. The Cowboys had the edge in the tiebreaker, so the Eagles became a wild-card team and lost at San Francisco in the wild-card game. The Jets lost their last game to Miami and finished 1–15, the worst record in franchise history.

That year I felt like it was more dysfunctional than anything else. A lot of phone calls being made, a lot of conversations being had. Everyone was just in survival mode at that point because we were getting our ass kicked every week. We were really undisciplined. And it didn't help that Kotite would just let the guys run wild.

Did I think it was always going to be like this? I did. I really did. I thought, "I'm never going to the playoffs. I'm never going to a contender for the playoffs." I knew some guys who were going to the Super Bowl. And I'm thinking, "They're going to the Super Bowl, I'm never even going to make the playoffs."

CHAPTER 5
A FRESH START

It was a good spot for me to be in all around. I was out of New York. I was back in a 4-3 defense. They were going to let me do what I do, rush the quarterback. I thought coming to the Eagles was perfect.

Hugh Douglas' first season as an Eagles was much like his first season with the Jets. Actually from a record standpoint it was exactly *like his first season with the Jets. Both teams finished 3–13. And Douglas, who had 10 sacks that rookie year in New York, recorded 12½ sacks his first season in Philadelphia. He was good. The team was bad.*

Philly was a playoff team (for two years in 1995 and 1996) and they were close in (1997). They thought they had their quarterback in Bobby Hoying. He had played well (at the end of the 1997 season). I was excited to be here. I was excited for a fresh start. I was excited to play for Ray Rhodes.

Playing for Ray meant everything to me, because it reminded me of playing for Coach Billy Joe (at Central State) again. It wasn't often in the NFL then to get to play for a Black head coach. I think it might have been the first for all of us (and as it turned out, it was also the last). I wanted to do well for him. You know, because we saw the way it was going and we didn't want to let him down.

He took a chance on trading for me. There was a lot being said about me coming out of New York. I still had that small-school thing. I didn't have a good year under Parcells, because of the defense we played. So there was a lot being said. I wanted to make sure I didn't make Ray look bad.

He didn't. The entire defense, with the exception of a couple of games, didn't. It was the offense that led to the three-win season and eventually Rhodes' demise. The Eagles scored a total of 161 points over their 16-game schedule. It doesn't take a Rhodes Scholar to figure out that's just a hair over 10 points per game. Only once did they score more than 20 points in a game, and that was in a 24–21 loss to Kansas City. And they were shut out three times, starting with the season opener at home against Seattle.

We just got trounced by Seattle. We did. It was awful. But after that we were in some games that if we would have had even a little bit of offense we could have won. We could have been all right. I remember (defensive coordinator) Emmitt Thomas would tell us before a game, "We're probably going to have to play a lot today." We knew it.

The Eagles managed just 174 yards of total offense in that opening day 38–0 loss to the Seahawks. They also committed three turnovers, including Seattle cornerback Shawn Springs' pick-six of a pass by Bobby Hoying on the Eagles second possession of the season. They followed that with a 17–12 loss to eventual NFC Champion Atlanta in a game they led at one point, 9–0. Then lost at Arizona, 17–3, at home to Kansas City, 24–21 (their highest scoring game of the season) and got embarrassed in Denver, 41–16, in a game that at one time was, 41–2. When it was 28–0 and the Eagles got a safety on a blocked punt, longtime football writer, the late Ron Reid, bellowed as only he could, "Thirteen more of those and they're right back in the game."

After that game, Rhodes told reporters, "It could have been worse. Coach (Mike) Shanahan called off the dogs."

When I came to Philadelphia—and I didn't realize it when I first got there because I was just happy to get out of New York—but it was real dysfunctional. Ray was on his way out. He was a lame-duck coach and I didn't know that when I first got there. Jeffrey Lurie (the owner) and Joe Banner (team president) were out at practice every day. So you kind of knew they were just waiting for the season to end to get rid of Ray. He would have had to have a real good season—playoffs at the least—to not get fired. And it didn't look like that was going to happen. It wasn't going well. It was like the Jets all over again.

The 0–5 Eagles got their first win of the season when they beat the 0–5 Washington Redskins at home, 17–12, in Week 6. In that game, veteran quarterback Rodney Peete, who replaced the ineffective Hoying, ran for one touchdown and threw for another. Only two wins would follow. The next was a 10–9 decision over the Detroit Lions in Week 10. Douglas had a key sack of

Charlie Batch on the Lions final possession and also drew a false-start penalty against Lions tackle David Sloan on that same possession. The game ended when Detroit kicker Jason Hanson missed from 58 yards out. And the final win came in Week 14 against Dick Vermeil's Rams. Koy Detmer threw for two touchdowns and Duce Staley ran for 99 yards in the 17–14 win.

We would change quarterbacks like every other week. It was Bobby, it was Peete, it was (Koy). It was crazy. We were in a bad spot, but we would fight. We would fight for Ray.

Ray was a good coach. He really was a good coach. You saw what he did his first two years there. He was just put in a bad spot. Ray was the coach and they were ready to move on for whatever reason and Ray wasn't going to be the guy moving forward. He was not going to be their guy.

It could have been different. If a trade that Rhodes was behind when he first got to Philadelphia had gone through the entire NFL landscape may have changed. Before Rhodes' first draft with the Eagles in 1995, the team engineered a trade with the Green Bay Packers for quarterback Mark Brunell, who Rhodes knew from his time in Green Bay as defensive coordinator under head coach Mike Holmgren. Brunell was Brett Favre's backup for the Packers, which means he never started a game and rarely played. He was about to become a free agent at the end of that 1995 season and the Packers were looking to get some draft-pick compensation before he left. He had been impressive enough in preseason that the Eagles were willing to part with a second- and fifth-round draft pick to acquire him. The deal was done to the extent that the Packers allowed the Eagles to work out a long-term deal with Brunell and his agent. And that's where the trouble started.

The team wanted a long-term deal, at least five years, if not six. The player and the agent wanted a three-year deal, so they could cash in again sooner. When the two sides couldn't compromise as the draft drew closer, the Packers backed off that deal and traded him instead to the expansion Jacksonville Jaguars for a third- and fifth-round pick. Brunell would play nine years for the Jaguars. He took them to the playoffs every year from 1996 to 1999, to the

AFC Championship Game in 1999, and went to three Pro Bowls along the way. Him at quarterback, with Ricky Watters at running back and Irving Fryar at wide receiver and that Rhodes-and-Thomas-coached defense and who knows what the Eagles may have accomplished. Instead they had Peete, Hoying, and both Detmer brothers. None of them were Brunell.

I got to know Mark Brunell when I was in Jacksonville (in 2003), he was coaching there then. I knew he was a good player. He was a good coach, too. And he was a really great guy.

The Eagles thought they solved their quarterback problem when they selected Hoying, out of Ohio State, in the third round of the 1996 NFL Draft. In his second year he came in and played well at the end of the season. Well enough that the back page of the Philadelphia Daily News *around Christmastime blared the headline, "Hoy to the World." In his first start he completed 26 of 38 passes for 276 yards in a tie with the Baltimore Ravens. He followed that debut with wins over the Pittsburgh Steelers, who went to the AFC Championship Game that season, and the Cincinnati Bengals. Against the Steelers he threw two first-quarter touchdowns to give the team a 14–0 lead that turned into a 23–20 win. And against the Bengals, Hoying, an Ohio native, outdueled a quarterback he admired watching, Boomer Esiason. He threw for 313 yards and four touchdowns and led the team on a game-winning field-goal drive in a 44–42 win. It may have been an omen, however, that the Eagles lost his last three starts to the Giants, the Falcons, and the Redskins.*

I remember when I got to Philly. The story was how they offered Bobby Hoying like five years, $25 million and Bobby (essentially) said: No, I'm not taking it. I want to get *paid*-paid. Then he had that horrible season (in 1998) and he was never heard from again. That was crazy. That was really crazy that that was the case. After that season he was never the same again.

Hoying's 1998 season was a disaster in every sense of the word. Not only did he turn down the contract offer, he went 1–6 as the Eagles starter before losing the job. He completed 50.9 percent of his passes, did not throw a touchdown, and threw nine interceptions. His quarterback rating was 45.6. No, the Eagles had not found their quarterback. He was in Jacksonville taking the Jaguars to the playoffs for the third straight season.

Bobby was in Jon Gruden's offense and Gruden made it simple for him. Gruden left (to become head coach of the Oakland Raiders) and everything was different. Then there was the whole Dana Bible thing.

During the offseason between 1997 and 1998 the Eagles hired two new coordinators. Dana Bible was hired to replace Gruden as offensive coordinator and John Harbaugh was hired as special teams coordinator to replace Joe Wessel. Let's just say they went 1-for-2.

I saw it right from early on in camp. I remember we're at practice and Ray said this verbatim. "We're not blitzing." We weren't really blitzing, but we were bringing the heat and killing the offense. And Ray said, "Come here ya'll. Ya'll have to stop bringing the heat, because this motherfucker can't handle this shit. Just play a vanilla defense, because this motherfucker, his shit ain't working. So just play vanilla." So we stopped. We called off the dogs in practice. We kind of saw it. They were bad, man. The offense was really bad. And Bible was part of why they were so bad.

From what I was told and what I saw, Ray never wanted Dana Bible. He wanted to hire Bill Musgrave. Bible was a Lurie or Banner hire. Ray wanted Musgrave, but somebody didn't want him. So they hired Bible and Ray hated it. The offense never had a chance.

In the middle of that season, a veteran Eagles offensive player told The Trenton (N.J.) Times *and* The Burlington County (N.J.) Times *that Bible, "Was the worst coach I've ever been around, in the pros, in college, in high school, in Pop Warner. He's the worst."*

Rhodes did add Musgrave, the former 49ers backup quarterback, to his staff during that 1998 season and eventually handed over the play-calling duties to him. By that point it hardly mattered. And the offense, coordinated by Bible and without a reliable quarterback, was basically damaged beyond repair.

There was only so much Musgrave could do. It's funny, because you're put in that situation, it was like the Eagles defense (in 2023). They bring in Matt Patricia late in the year when the defense (under coordinator Sean Desai) was playing so poorly. And I remember (Patricia) told me, "I'm running someone else's defense." It wasn't his defense, or in Musgrave's case, it wasn't his offense. And now you're also asking the guys to change what they were taught from the beginning of training camp. That's not fair to the guys, either. You can't do it. So you try to pare it down as much as you can and take it from there. That's basically what we did. But it was just a mess.

How bad was it between Rhodes and the front office? The head coach brought in quarterback Kerry Collins, a first-round draft pick in 1995 who had been released by the Carolina Panthers for a workout one Tuesday during the season. The front office refused to sign him. Collins later signed with the New Orleans Saints, and then the New York Giants, who he took to the Super Bowl in 2000. The die had been cast and for Rhodes it came up snake eyes.

There was nothing Ray could do (to save his job). At that point it was over. And we all knew it. They (Rhodes and his staff) knew it, too. They knew they were gone and Emmitt used to tell us, "Hey, you have to put out some good tape for the next guy. You're basically an independent contractor."

From the outside it appeared some of the players gave up on the season. As the losses piled up, some tried as Thomas suggested to put out some good tape. Others didn't.

I can tell you this. I don't know about the offense, because I wasn't on offense. Tra Thomas (rookie left tackle and future Pro Bowl player) played well, I know that. But there were other guys, (right tackle) Richard Cooper got Reggie-itis and didn't play against Green Bay, because he didn't want to face Reggie White. I remember on defense, playing for

Emmitt and Ray, no one on that side of the ball wanted to let those guys down. We played hard every Sunday. We didn't win a lot and we got our ass kicked some games, but we played hard. That was a fact.

Despite the record, the lack of an offense, the quarterback carousel, and Rhodes being let down and eventually fired. There was groundwork being put down for what would turn out to be a bright future for the team. Oh, and Douglas tied a team record that still stands almost 30 years later. Against the San Diego Chargers, Douglas recorded 4½ sacks of quarterback Ryan Leaf. Clyde Simmons had 4½ sacks of Troy Aikman in Dallas back in 1991. And the two, as of 2025, still share the record for most sacks in a game by an Eagle. The late, great Reggie White? The team's all-time sack leader, had four sacks in a game three times, but never 4½.

I was all over that left tackle (the Chargers John Jackson). I was talking a lot of shit to that left tackle. I kept telling him, "It's a long day for you." But the unfortunate thing was we still lost. A reporter asked me after the game how did it feel to get 4½ sacks? I told him it don't feel good because we lost. You know it's funny you look back at things when you get old and some of the things you were able to accomplish and you're like, "Wow." When you're in the moment you don't really think about it."

Douglas' first year with the Eagles was hardly a success on the field. Off the field and in the locker room he did get to know the teammates who would go a long way in both his and the team's future, however.

We were a real eclectic group of players that year.

Hollis (Thomas, the big defensive tackle) was one of the first cats I hung out when I got there. We kind of gravitated to each other because we were both from small schools, so we had that in common. I'm from Central State and he was from Northern Illinois. And he was just starting to come into his own as a player that year, too.

I remember (running back) Charle Garner being there, too. I think that might have been his last year there. He put Duce (Staley) on, because Charlie would hardly take any reps in practice. So Duce took most of the reps. Charlie would run the ball one time, and be like, "Yo, Duce, get out here, come get me." And Duce was working. He was basically our whole offense that year. Duce was that dude. It's like you're always told never let the guy behind you get a chance to show what he can do. That was Duce. Charlie let him in and he went out there and took advantage of the situation.

Troy Vincent was our leader. He's always been a leader. He still is. I think he's going to be the NFL Commissioner one day. Troy was laid back. But he was a leader. You listened to Troy. Even though he wasn't that old, he was the elder statesman.

(Brian Dawkins) wasn't "Dawk" yet, but he was on his way. When I got to the Eagles, and this is the God's honest truth, I thought I was the best player on the defense and then I saw Dawk. I remember one game we were playing the Giants and Tiki Barber ran a draw play right up the middle. I went upfield and I'm chasing and I'm running behind Tiki and all of a sudden Tiki just dropped to the ground. Like just dropped and when he did I looked up and all I saw was a black visor and the No. 20. Brian Dawkins put me to sleep. I saw the video afterwards and Dawk was praying over me. He was praying because he thought he killed me. He knocked me out. But I knew right then, he could play. Right then I started looking at him differently. This cat right here can play. The thing about Dawk, too, was he was real quiet all week, you hardly heard from him. But on game day he was different. Man, he was different. Being in the huddle with him, like I said, you never wanted to let Ray down, you really didn't want to let Dawk down.

I played with a really good group of guys. You see guys now and even though it's been some time, it's like we didn't miss a beat. I saw Bobby Taylor not that long ago in Louisiana. It had been a while since I had seen him. But it was like we were back together all over again. Time doesn't matter when you're with your friends. They're like brothers. When you see them, you're happy to see them.

CHAPTER 6

WHAT'S NEXT?

I told Ray, "Wherever you go, I want to go with you."

He said, "Hugh, you're not coming with me. They're not letting you go. You'll be all right."

The inevitable happened December 28, 1998, three days after Christmas and a day after the Eagles lost for a team-record 13th time in one season. Ray Rhodes was fired as head coach. From the NFL's Coach of the Year in 1995 when he took a team that had suffered the greatest collapse in NFL history a year before to a win in the playoffs to the embarrassment of the 1998 season, the losingest in franchise history, it was a tumultuous four years in Eagles history.

I knew something was up. We all knew something was up. Something was definitely happening when Jeff (Lurie, the owner) and Joe (Banner, the team president) were around every day. They were out at practice every day. They were always around. So you knew something was happening. They were out there every day. There was a conversation every day. It was over for Ray.

When most head coaches get fired in any professional sport inevitably some of the players turn on them and bad mouth them on their way out of the door. "He didn't do this. He couldn't do that. We were outcoached." That didn't happen with the 1998 Eagles. Not one of the 53 men on the roster, at least publicly, had a bad word to say about Rhodes after the Eagles decided to let him go. Listen, the players weren't happy about 3–13, but to a man none of them blamed it on Rhodes.

Nobody was going to blame Ray, especially the guys on the defense. There was blame to go around, but we didn't point fingers. That's not what this team did.

Fingers did start to point as to what coach would replace Rhodes as the Eagles next head coach. There were four announced candidates, although in reality there were only three—Pittsburgh Steelers defensive coordinator Jim Haslett, Jacksonville Jaguars offensive coordinator Chris Palmer, and Green Bay Packers quarterbacks coach Andy Reid. Oakland Raiders defensive coordinator Willie Shaw was also interviewed, but for the most part that was just to satisfy the NFL's Rooney Rule, which states that a team must interview a minority candidate when it's hiring a head coach. Shaw is Black.

Haslett appeared to be the favorite. A year earlier the Eagles hired Tom Modrak to be its de facto general manager. Modrak worked in the Steelers front office for years before joining the Eagles and when he was hired the team wanted everyone to know they were going to follow the Pittsburgh blueprint to success. (When they hired Rhodes, who was the 49ers defensive coordinator, they let it be known they were going to follow the San Francisco blueprint to success.) If they wanted to be the Steelers, why not get their defensive coordinator? And if he and Modrak weren't close from working together, they also both attended the same college Indiana (Pa.) University. Was it a slam dunk? We'll get to that.

We didn't really know what was going on as far as who they were going to hire. Some of the guys talked about it, but it's not like they involved us in the decision. What we did hear the most was it was going to be Haslett.

Palmer was an interesting candidate as well. He grew up in Connecticut and was the head coach at Boston University in 1988 and 1989. Remember, Lurie and Banner are both Boston natives. Palmer was also an assistant coach for the New England Patriots from 1993 to 1996, serving first as wide receivers coach and then quarterbacks coach for Bill Parcells. The Patriots were Lurie's and Banner's favorite team before Lurie bought the Eagles. And it was the Patriots that Lurie wanted to buy before he purchased the Eagles in 1994. So Palmer had all of that going for him. He also did a good job as Jacksonville's offensive coordinator, helping the 1995 expansion team to the playoffs as OC in both 1997 and 1998, while helping develop a quarterback named Mark Brunell into a Pro Bowl player.

Reid was the least known of the three. But word had begun to spread in league circles that Brett Favre's quarterback coach was an up-and-comer. He never served as Mike Holmgren's coordinator—that was Sherman

Lewis—but it was Holmgren's offense anyway and he called the plays. So it really wasn't that big of a deal who had the title of OC. Reid had the blessing of Favre, who had already won three MVP Awards and a Super Bowl.

While Palmer and Reid were interesting candidates, Haslett seemed to be the choice. When he held a mini press conference after his interview with the team, it almost appeared as if he had the job. Because maybe he did.

When he was the defensive coordinator for the Washington Redskins (2010–14) I saw him and I got talking to him. I remember him telling me, "I had that job. But that fucking Joe Banner kept calling my phone every day. He kept bothering me. I just stopped answering the call."

The Eagles defensive players—a unit which pretty much stayed intact under the new regime—would have welcomed Haslett. Douglas especially looked forward to playing in a Steelers-style defense.

I was excited. I grew up liking the Pittsburgh Steelers. When I met Mean Joe Greene and he knew who I was, that was one of my greatest highlights. So we're hiring the defensive coordinator from Pittsburgh, yeah I was excited. I thought, "This is going to be good. We have a good defense. We're getting a good defensive coach. All we need now is to get the offense figured out, get a good quarterback." And with the second pick (in the draft), we were probably going to get someone pretty good.

Douglas envisioned himself and Mike Mamula being the Eastern Pennsylvania version of the Steelers twin pass-rush specialists Kevin Greene and Greg Lloyd. Hollis Thomas would have fit fine as the nose tackle in the 3-4 scheme. And the secondary had three future Pro Bowl players in cornerbacks Troy Vincent and Bobby Taylor and safety Brian Dawkins. A tweak here and there and the Eagles defense could have been every bit as good as the Steelers. Maybe even better.

We thought for sure he was getting the job and when it didn't happen we didn't know why. Although as it turned out it worked out pretty well.

Banner, who had messed up the Mark Brunell trade a few years earlier, had gotten in the way again. Only it did work out in the Eagles' favor this time. Haslett returned to Pittsburgh for another year as their defensive coordinator and then became the head coach of the New Orleans Saints in 2000. In six years as the Saints coach he had a 45–51 record, that included just one play-off appearance (2000) and a 3–13 final record that ended his tenure in 2005.

Palmer ended up in Cleveland with the "new" Cleveland Browns, who were re-entering the league in 1999. He lasted just two years with the new franchise, going 2–14 his first year and 3–13 his second year before being fired and heading to Houston as Dom Capers offensive coordinator for another expansion franchise, the Houston Texans.

Exactly two weeks after Rhodes was fired, January 11, 1999, the Eagles announced that Reid was their next head coach. Ironically, the Green Bay Packers announced that same day that Rhodes was being hired to replace Holmgren, who had left Green Bay to become head coach and general manager of the Seattle Seahawks.

We didn't know anything after the Haslett thing fell apart. Then they told us they were hiring the quarterbacks coach from Green Bay. Who? Yeah, we're getting Brett Favre's quarterback coach. Who gives a fuck about that? We didn't give a shit about Brett Favre or his quarterback coach. We heard Andy Reid got the job and we were like, "Who the hell is Andy Reid?"

CHAPTER 7
BIG RED

Andy came in like Suge Knight at his first Death Row meeting. He came in and he was matter of fact. "This is what we are going to do and we are going to be a good football team." He was talking real positive. And that got us excited.

Andy Reid became the 19th head coach of the Philadelphia Eagles when he was hired January 11, 1999. Fourteen years later he left as the franchise's leader in both regular-season (130) and playoff (10) wins. The hire was considered a bit of a surprise when it happened. Eagles owner Jeffrey Lurie and team president Joe Banner, however, were impressed by Reid during his interview with the team and how prepared he was to become a head coach.

Again, Big Red was a quarterbacks coach, not even a coordinator. Compared to Jim Haslett, what the hell are we getting? We had a really good defense, now what are we going to do. (Andy) had no pedigree. He had no résumé so to speak.

Reid's claim to fame was being Brett Favre's quarterback coach with the Green Bay Packers, a title he inherited from Steve Mariucci, who was the Packers quarterback coach before becoming the head coach at the University of California and then head coach of the San Francisco 49ers. The Packers, under head coach Mike Holmgren, were turning out head coach after head coach, including both Ray Rhodes, who Reid replaced with the Eagles, and former Eagles offensive coordinator Jon Gruden, who had become the head coach of the Oakland Raiders a year before Reid took over the Eagles. Maybe this Reid guy, despite his inexperience, was going to be okay.

We get to training camp and there was nothing like it. Not saying Ray's training camps or the ones with the Jets were easy, but Andy's training camp was brutal. *Brutal.* He's still new and we don't know him or what direction he wanted us to go. All we knew was he was working us like dogs. He was killing us. It was like, "What is he doing?"

He told us we're going to go really hard for three straight days. So it's like the second day and we don't know what the hell is going on at this point. We're out there banging. Just banging and banging every day, every practice. We're frustrated. We're hot. We're mad. And I remember saying, "This motherfucker don't know what he's doing."

Andy heard me and he says, "Stop your bitching. Don't you see you're getting better." When he said that a light went on for me. He was trying to break us to see who he could count on and who he couldn't count on when the season started. After I said what I said, he called a meeting and he said, "Listen, we're only going to do this a couple of more days. But I need to see who's with me. I need to figure out who I can depend on in the long run." And then it all started to make sense.

It didn't take all that long for Reid to figure out who would stay and who would go. And some who went were big names. Running back Charlie Garner, quarterbacks Rodney Peete and Bobby Hoying, tackle Richard Cooper, and wide receiver Irving Fryar were gone from the offense. Former first-round pick defensive end Jon Harris and cornerback/returner Allen Rossum were left off the defense. And that was just in his first year.

I thought Andy was crazy. He was getting rid of guys one by one. I remember one of the first moves he did was cut George Hegamin—or demoted him and then cut him. He had played in the Super Bowl (with Dallas) and he's getting rid of him. We were like, "Damn, this mother is cold blooded." But he was weeding cats out. The ones he cut early, he wanted to see what other guys were going to do, wanted to see our reactions.

Before Hegamin was released, Reid embarrassed him in front of the media. The Eagles, who ran relatively closed practices, opened practice that day to the media, or at least the part they wanted to be seen. That was to watch Hegamin, who had drawn Reid's wrath, push a blocking sled up and down the practice field. The head coach was sending a message. And it was received.

Andy was in a position and a situation where it was his first head coaching job. He comes in and he doesn't know us from a can of paint. This is his one opportunity to be a head coach in the NFL. He's either going to make it, or he's not. So he's trying to right this ship because he knows what it could mean for him. So he's going with penitentiary rules.

He's running an asylum and he's the warden. He's trying to figure out who's getting totally into lock step and who he has to get rid of. As we got to know him and he got to know us he changed a little bit. He would tell those corny jokes. He became a little more down to Earth.

Reid's first staff turned out to rival some of the coaching staffs he was on under Holmgren in Green Bay. Longtime assistants Jim Johnson (defense) and Rod Dowhower (offense) were his two coordinators. He kept the Ray Rhodes–hired John Harbaugh as his special teams coach. And then added the likes of Ron Rivera (linebackers), Leslie Frazier (defensive backs), Steve Spagnuolo (defensive assistant), Brad Childress (quarterbacks), David Culley (wide receivers), Pat Shurmur (tight ends), and Sean McDermott (personnel assistant). Those last eight all became NFL head coaches at one point in their careers.

He brought in some elder statesmen in Rod and Jim. Those guys helped him a lot, especially that first season.

Johnson, who died from cancer after the 2008 season, became known as one of the best defensive coordinators in the league in his 10 years with Reid and the Eagles. Douglas saw it first hand.

Jim came in and one thing he did was he kept the defense simple. The best thing about Jim, he was able to adapt to the players he had.

I remember early on he had this one defense he wanted to run. And I kept messing it up. I kept running underneath, but I was making the play. Jim is like, "That's not how we run it. Run it again." So I would run it again and I would see the action of the tackle and I would go underneath and I would make the play. And I did it like two or three times in a row. And Tommy (Brasher, the defensive line coach) is like, "Damn it, Douglas, you keep messing up the play."

So we're in the meeting the next day and Jim said we're going to put this stunt in called "The Wing Stunt" and we're going to do it out of this formation. (Defensive lineman) Brandon Whiting said, "No, Hugh keeps fucking up the defense." So they called me the founder of the Wing Stunt. Because I kept messing up the play, but it worked.

With Jim we got after the quarterback. We really got after the quarterback. We blitzed. We blitzed a lot. We blitzed on run downs. We didn't care. Our thing was we might give up some yards, but we bowed our neck at the 20. It played to my strength as a pass rusher. That's what I wanted to do was get after the quarterback. We weren't that big, so we were always moving. We did slants, stunts, whatever it took. Jim put us in a position where we were always on the move. We would run under, over, and we always brought some kind of pressure.

Reid's staff, especially Johnson, turned out to be a strength, especially in the years to follow. So too was his first-ever, first-round draft pick, quarterback Donovan McNabb out of Syracuse.

There was a lot of controversy surrounding the selection, but the Eagles and Reid got it right. Texas running back Ricky Williams was the popular pick among fans, especially a certain group led by Philadelphia sports talk radio station WIP. A group of 30 were at that 1999 Draft and booed loudly when the McNabb selection was made. ESPN still plays the Eagles fans booing their quarterback every year prior to the draft. And McNabb wasn't the only top-ranked quarterback. He was one of five to get selected in the first 12 picks of that 1999 Draft. Tim Couch (Cleveland), Akili Smith (Cincinnati), Daunte Culpepper (Minnesota), and Cade McNown (Chicago) were the other four.

The draft comes and there's a lot of talk about Tim Couch (who went No. 1 to Cleveland) and Donovan McNabb. (The Eagles had the No. 2 pick.) One of our scouts was telling us all about Donovan and that we're probably going to take him with our pick. I'm excited about that, because he's a quarterback. That's something we don't have. We're going to get a quarterback. So to me that's a good thing. Then I watched some of his highlights and it was, "Okay, this guy is pretty good. He can play."

We heard about the Ricky Williams stuff, most of it was on the radio. We didn't need a running back. We needed a quarterback. We *really* needed a quarterback. If you watched us play the year before you saw how much we needed a quarterback. I mean, you have to get a quarterback when you need a quarterback or you're never going to win. We had a good running back in Duce (Staley). We didn't have a quarterback.

Donovan was good. Donovan had some legs. He could run. He was in that Mike Vick vein of running quarterbacks. And he had a big arm, too. Donovan could throw the ball. You could argue about his accuracy, but Donovan could throw that thing.

McNabb sat early in the season as the team took its lumps with veteran Doug Pederson, who, as irony would have it, would come back and coach the Eagles to their first Super Bowl win 18 years later. Pederson won two of his nine starts before giving way to the rookie who would win two of his six starts. Koy Detmer started the other game in place of an injured McNabb and went 1–0.

Doug Pederson was the quarterback for the time. But Andy was slowly working Donovan in little by little. You could see what was happening there. We knew what was happening. He didn't want to throw (McNabb) to the wolves. He wanted him to watch and learn. When Donovan got his chance, everything changed. You saw that. Say what you want about Donovan, but he brought a swagger that we needed, that the offense needed. He had the right attitude for that team.

Reid's first year looked a lot like Rhodes' last year when the team was 3–11 with two weeks to go. Wins those final two games against the New England Patriots and the Super Bowl–bound St. Louis Rams may have been a sign of things to come.

If drafting McNabb before the 1999 season was step one in turning the Eagles from a last-place team in the NFC East into a nine-time playoff team and six-time division winner from 2000 to 2010 under Reid, step two was a big free agent signing the following year. During the 2000 free agent period the Eagles made Tennessee Titans right tackle Jon Runyan the then highest paid right tackle in the league and paired him with 1998 first-round draft pick, left tackle Tra Thomas. Those bookend tackles to protect their franchise quarterback were the keys to the offense's success.

Tra was a good player, a damn good left tackle. Then Runyan comes in and he changes everything. That first training camp, he was getting in a fight every other day, sometimes every day and sometimes more than one. He brought out a lot of attitude to a lot of guys. Jon Runyan, I love him to death, but he's one of the nastiest motherfuckers I've ever been around. The funny thing, he didn't say a lot off the field. He was kind of quiet. But on the field he brought that nastiness. It was like, something's not right with this guy. He reveled in that shit—punishing fools, doing dirty shit. It was wild. I remember one of the first training camp practices and him and Trot got into a fight. It was classic. But Jon Runyan, he made us a better team.

That second year, Reid and Douglas, in their own unique way, began what has become a lifetime bond. It started with them getting on different busses and Douglas giving Reid his nickname.

I still keep in touch with Big Red. I text him all the time. I root for the Kansas City Chiefs unless they're playing the Eagles.

That second year I wasn't allowed to get on the bus (to the game) with Andy. I had this way of getting ready for a game. It was my way. It was kind of loud. And Andy said, "Listen, whatever you do, do whatever you have to do to get ready on Sunday." It got to the point, if Andy didn't hear me he thought something was wrong. I would get on the bus and I would just make noise for no reason. At first Andy thought something was wrong. He would say, "You okay? We got a game. Calm down."

And I would tell him, "This is how I get ready for a game." So after a while I had to get on a different bus. If I was on the bus first and Andy got on it, he would cringe. And I would have to get off the bus and get on a different one. Then I figured out he would always be on the first bus, so I would just get on the last bus.

And then "Big Red" was born.

He had that big-ass spiky red hair. He would come in with that scowl on his face, wearing his Green Bay Super Bowl ring. I would say look at his big ass with that big hair. He's Big Red. I started calling him "Big Red" like the chewing gum. He was one of those fiery redheads. I thought "Big Red" just fit.

Reid did too. He took to the nickname rather well.

What choice did he have? I mean really, what choice did he have?

Reid knew what he had in Douglas, a Pro Bowl, pass-rushing defensive end who was a terror on the field and a good teammate in the locker room. So while he would shake his head at times, he just let Hugh be Hugh.

We would be in practice and I'd be yelling or screaming about something and Andy would try to ignore me. I would scream out something like, "I'm so horny."

And he would try not to laugh. But he would shake his head and think, "This guy is crazy." He would tell me, "There's something wrong with you, there is something seriously wrong with you." I was loud and boisterous. But that's just me. That's how I would get ready. I spoke my mind. I still do to this day.

As successful as Reid was as head coach of the Eagles, he left after a terrible 2012 season where the Eagles finished 4–12. Five trips to the NFC Championship Game resulted in just one Super Bowl appearance and a loss to the New England Patriots. When he left the big market of Philadelphia for a smaller, more laid-back Kansas City things changed. Since arriving in Kansas City as head coach of the Chiefs, Reid has won, won, and won some more. He's taken the Chiefs to five Super Bowls and has won three. A very good coach in Philadelphia, Reid has become a Hall of Fame coach in Kansas City.

I saw some of Andy's flaws. People in Philadelphia, some of them anyway, don't like Andy because he never brought home a Super Bowl championship. But you know Andy learned from his mistakes. One of his blind spots was he never wanted to go get a big-time wide receiver until he got (Terrell Owens). Then shit changed. In his early days he didn't adjust well. His first couple years it was his way or the highway. Since then he's adapted.

From the perspective as a beat writer and later a columnist who was there for all 14 of Reid's years with the Eagles, there was never a better coach on Wednesday through Friday. His practices were organized, crisp, and as well-run as anyone's. He broke down the other team and what they did and couldn't do as well as any coach I've ever witnessed. When his game plan worked, the Eagles would not just win, but win in routs. When it didn't, however, and the opposition came up with something unplanned, Reid struggled at times. That doesn't seem to happen, or at least not very often, in Kansas City.

He learned. Having a quarterback like (Kansas City's) Patrick Mahomes helps, too. Listen, Donovan was a good quarterback, but he wasn't Patrick Mahomes. Who is? And Kansas City isn't Philly. It's a totally different situation for him there, I mean, Philly is just a different place.

And Reid has become a different person as well as a different (and better) coach. Those commercials you see him on all the time now, Snickers, State Farm, etc. That never happened even on local TV in Philadelphia. It just wasn't him. It's funny because I knew people in Green Bay and when Reid was hired I was told how much I would like him and how good he would be from a media standpoint. That he was funny, glib, easygoing. We rarely, if ever, saw that side of him. Instead he was, well, boring, especially in the aftermath of coaches like Buddy Ryan and Ray Rhodes who proceeded him in Philadelphia.

It's amazing how much he changed (in Kansas City). He's more playful. I guess winning Super Bowls will do that for you.

Before the Chiefs played the Eagles in 2023 in Kansas City I went out for the game and went a couple days early. I went to a Chiefs practice and saw Big Red. Here he is driving a T Rex, a Ram truck. Back in Philly he would always drive a Suburban or something like that. Now, the T Rex has some giddy up. So I was like, "Big Red, you're driving a T Rex?"

He says, "Hugh, it's so fast." He was like a little kid. He changed so much. He's back to being the guy he was in Green Bay before he got to Philly.

CHAPTER 8

AN ARM AND A LEG (1999)

You're an afterthought. You're definitely an afterthought. You see the team playing. You see the guys going through it and there's nothing you can do, nothing. You're a liability at that point. You're not an asset.

Andy Reid's debut season as the Eagles head coach was not a good one for the Eagles, and especially for Hugh Douglas. The Eagles finished 5–11 under Reid, and in last place in the NFC East. Douglas missed two games early in the season with a knee injury and the final 10 games of the season with a torn biceps injury.

Andy had a plan. He had us fighting. We, or they, were playing hard. The thing I thought was special about Andy was that you could see what he was doing. We just needed some more talent on offense. Duce (running back Staley) was doing his thing. Duce was no joke. And we had Chad Lewis at tight end. Now Chad turned the corner. He was here and got cut. He got cut again by someone else (the Rams), came back, and became a big part of our offense. He was a big part of Donovan's (McNabb) success.

But offenses, especially back then, you needed time to see what they could do. And unfortunately for us we had a bunch of young guys on offense. Our wide receivers were Charles Johnson and Torrance Small and we had Doug (quarterback Pederson), he was okay. He knew the offense (from being with Reid in Green Bay). But Doug was just a stop gap. He wasn't the guy. Everyone knew he wasn't the guy. So we still didn't have a whole lot on offense. It was Chad and Duce and then Chad got hurt, too.

The Eagles began the season 0–2, although Douglas had a sack in both of the losses at home to Arizona and Tampa Bay. The opening day loss to Arizona in Reid's first game as a head coach was especially excruciating. The Eagles led 21–0 at the end of the first quarter and 24–6 at halftime. The Cardinals outscored them 19–0 in the second half to win 25–24 on a 31-yard field goal by Chris Jacke with four seconds left, who Reid knew well from their days together in Green Bay. At the two-minute warning, the Eagles still led 24–22 and faced a third-and-4 at their 49-yard line. Reid decided to throw long and Pederson went to Brian Finneran, an undrafted rookie free agent from Villanova, down the left sideline. The ball went off the rookie's hands and into those of Cardinals safety Kwamie Lassiter, who returned it to the Eagles 43-yard line. Arizona quarterback Jake Plummer competed a 13-yard pass to the 30 and ran for 17 yards to give Jacke a chip-shot field goal. Finneran was released two weeks later and went on to have a decent nine-year career with the Atlanta Falcons. In that game, Staley actually ran for more yards (111 on 21 carries) than Pederson had passing (91 on 12 completions in 26 attempts).

I remember that first game against Arizona. Yeah, Andy was pissed. We should have won that game. But Andy was upset, he ended up cutting Brian. He kind of made him the scapegoat. I mean he should have caught that pass, but damn that was cold. Then Brian went on to Atlanta and did pretty well. He had a nice career for the Falcons.

The 19–5 loss to Tampa also at home in Week 2 may have been worse than the blown game against the Cardinals. Reid's offense managed just nine first downs and 150 total yards. Pederson was 12-for-19 for 100 yards before Eagles fans saw rookie Donovan McNabb, the No. 2 overall pick of the 1999 Draft, for the first time. They may have wished they hadn't when he went 4-for-11 for 26 yards and got sacked six times. Adding injury to insult, Douglas went down with a knee injury.

I forget exactly what happened, or how it happened. But I remember it was my knee. I know I had to wear a knee brace after that.

Reports were that it was a partial tear of a ligament in his left leg and Douglas would be out anywhere from four to six weeks. He missed just two games—losses on the road to Buffalo, 26–0, and to the New York Giants, 16–15.

I know what they said. I wanted to come back. I was trying to play. I just thought that was going to be a pretty significant season for us and for me. And then there's that thing about you get hurt every year you play. I had to play through that. I wanted to be re-li-able.

Douglas came back and the 0–4 Eagles put together consecutive wins against Dallas, 13–10, and at Chicago, 20–16. The Douglas-inspired defense won the Cowboys game with three forced turnovers. Cornerbacks Troy Vincent and Bobby Taylor both intercepted Troy Aikman and linebacker William

Thomas forced and recovered an Emmitt Smith fumble. There was some irony in Reid's first win coming against Dallas. After the Eagles previous two head coaches, Rich Kotite and Ray Rhodes, went a combined 5–13 against the Cowboys, Reid would go 17–12 against the NFC East–rival Cowboys. Pederson, who threw the winning touchdown pass with 1:07 left to beat the Cowboys, had his best game as an Eagle in the win over the Bears. He completed 22 of 38 passes for 228 yards with two touchdowns and no interceptions. The defense was again the key, however, with four sacks and two interceptions of Bears rookie quarterback Cade McNown. In that win at Soldier Field, Douglas' season ended with a snap, a crackle, and …

I just heard it go pop. And I felt the muscle move. It rolled up. It was a torn biceps and that was that. At that point I just needed to learn more about my body. I went to the Eagles doctor. Now remember that was just my second year there. The doctor says we can do the surgery …. And I remember I said, "No, Doc, I don't trust you. I don't know you like that." I had the surgery in New York with the Jets doctor. For me it was a time where you had to be comfortable with the doctor. And I just felt more comfortable with the doctor in New York.

Out for the season and still not totally entrenched in the Philadelphia life, Douglas went home to Atlanta to sulk and more importantly get better.

I'm going to miss the rest of the season and I was bummed out about that. I went home to Atlanta. There was no reason for me to be there. I went home and tried to get healthy and get ready for next season. What people don't realize is when you're hurt like that and you're out for the season there's not a lot you can do. I mean there's really nothing you can do. It's different if there's a chance you can come back. Like (Eagles defensive end) Brandon Graham (in 2024), he was able to come back and he did. But I tore my biceps and back then with a torn biceps, you were just out. They had to take my bicep tendon and drill it through my bone and it had to set and that took a while. Then I had to strengthen the muscle and that took a while.

Graham came back not only through modern medicine, but because the Eagles were able to make it to the Super Bowl after the 2024 season. The Super Bowl was his first game back. The 1999 Eagles were not going to the Super Bowl, or even the playoffs.

The team was fighting I know that. (Linebacker) Ike (Reese) had to play some defensive end and he hated it. They were kind of going defensive end by committee because I wasn't there.

After the modest two-game win streak, the Eagles lost three straight. They beat Washington, then lost four straight, including rematches with Dallas and Washington. Douglas watched from afar and set his sights on the 2000 season.

What do you do? You stew, you wait, and you get healthy. At that point I'm just trying to figure it all out and what I need to do to get healthy and stay healthy. It's, "Okay, Hugh, you're getting a little older, you don't want to be the guy who is always hurt."

Better health all around came about through the aid of a trainer he heard about through other players in the league. That work not just got him healthy it set the tone for the rest of his career.

I forgot who put me on to him. But I got put on to (Hall of Fame tight end) Shannon Sharpe's trainer, The Ropeman, Ty Felder. I was like, "Why do they call him 'Ropeman'?" They said, "It's because he gets you tight." I went to Ropeman's gym in Atlanta. I would work out with Rope for hours every day and then go to the track and work out more. Every day. He would have us running sprints, gassers, all types of stuff every day.

You would be in the gym and Rope would say, "Give me 100 reps on the bench."

I would be, "What do you mean 100 reps?" What he was doing was he was building muscle endurance. He had a crazy workout. And that's what we did every day. It was tough. It was hard. It was grueling. But when I came back I was ready to rock and roll. Rope was the trainer that helped me stay healthy. He taught me how to eat better, too. I started eating like a bodybuilder. Started eating a lot of protein, foods that would help fuel my body. I wasn't eating right before. So when I came back I knew what to eat. I knew to put the right things in my body. Before I was eating all kinds of stuff, chicken fingers, french fries, all kinds of shit. I changed my diet and was able to stay healthy. Well, you're always banged up in this league, but I stayed functional. Rope used to be a bodybuilder and then all of a sudden he started training athletes. And he knew about nutrition, he would tell me to eat steaks, vegetables, good things. All that information and all that work it really helped me out tremendously.

While Douglas got better, so did the Eagles. After falling to 3–11 as the offense's struggles continued and the defense began to wear out, they managed to come back and win their final two games of the season at home. The Eagles beat a New England team that just missed the playoffs by a game, 24–9, and beat the eventual Super Bowl Champion Rams, 38–31. Koy Detmer, subbing for an injured McNabb, completed just 10 passes in the win over the Patriots but three were for touchdowns, two to Torrance Small. The Eagles defense sacked New England quarterback Drew Bledsoe six times, three by Mike Mamula, and intercepted him four times, two by Troy Vincent. In the win over the Rams, McNabb returned and threw three touchdown passes to Chad Lewis, Duce Staley, and Small. The defense sacked Rams quarterbacks Kurt Warner and Joe Germaine five times and forced seven turnovers, including pick-sixes by Mike Mamula and Al Harris.

Everyone talked about those last two games. Even when we got to camp the next year we were talking about those two games. The bottom line is we played better under Coach Reid. We had more direction. You knew it was only a matter of time. You saw it coming. You saw it at the end of the season. We were coming.

CHAPTER 9

FIRSTS: PLAYOFFS AND THE PRO BOWL

Making the playoffs in 2000 was one of the greatest feelings in the world. You know, everyone's not playing this weekend. That was significant for me. There are a lot of great football players who have never been to the playoffs. There are a lot of great ones who never saw a playoff game. So that was one of the greatest feelings in the world for me, because it was an experience I didn't know I would ever have.

After going through a 4–28 first two years with the New York Jets and an 8–24 first two seasons with the Eagles (there was also a 9–7 season with the Jets, but it was the worst year of his career from a playing standpoint), Hugh Douglas was headed to the postseason for the first time. He was also headed to the Pro Bowl, but more on that later.

We were getting to where we wanted to be as a team. And it was different in Philly at that time because we were winning. And you know everyone in Philly was always an Eagles fan, but now they had something to be proud of again. When I came to Philly it was cool, but it wasn't as cool as when we started winning. There was more respect. It was fun.

Andy Reid's second year as head coach of the Eagles was much better than his first and a healthy Hugh Douglas was just one of the reasons why. The Eagles finished 11–5, a game behind the New York Giants in the NFC East, but good enough to claim the Conference's top wild-card berth. The 11 wins were the most for the team since 1992, when it also went 11–5. Douglas recorded a career-best 15 sacks, which ranked fourth best in the league and just two off league leader Le'Roi Glover of the New Orleans Saints.

So it's funny how this all played out for me. It's the beginning of training camp. I just came back from being injured the year before and (defensive line coach) Tommy Brasher calls me in his office and says, "Hey, Douglas, it's about that time."

I said, "Time for what?"

He said, "Time for you take your game to the next level. Time for you to make the Pro Bowl. You need to make that happen. It's time. You're a good player, but it's time to take it to the next level."

A little help from a new teammate helped that cause in a roundabout way.

That's the year we drafted (defensive tackle) Corey Simon (with the sixth overall pick). His arrogant ass came in from Florida State. He's one of the best defensive players in the draft, and he's one of the best ever from Florida State. I'm hearing about how his locker is enshrined there in their Hall of Fame or whatever. Corey is our first-round draft pick and he's there kind of full of himself and I'm walking through the training room and Corey says to me, "Yo, let me go ahead and get that number 53, because you're not going to take it to the Pro Bowl." I'll never forget that. Corey pissed me off. He's a rookie and he's saying that to me. I'm thinking, "Has this motherfucker lost his mind?" I can't beat him up, because he's my teammate, so I just ate it. I didn't say anything.

Douglas would let his play talk for him. Well, except for during pregame. That started before the season opener in Dallas and Reid made sure it continued all season.

Everybody's talking about the start of the season. And everyone's excited. We had won those last two games last year and we want it to carry over. Plus, we're playing Dallas and all of that. So we're getting ready for the Cowboys and right before the game they made a switch on the defensive line. Corey had been playing next to me (at right defensive tackle) and they switched him from right to left. The story behind that was it was the first game of the season and his first NFL game and they didn't want him to go against (Dallas Pro Bowl guard) Larry Allen. They were afraid Larry Allen would snatch his soul. That was the first salvo that they were worried about Dallas. They were scared. Then it was how hot it was going to be in Dallas. It's going to be over 100 degrees. I'm hearing this all week, right? Now, Dallas had kicked our ass a lot, so there's that, but I'm getting tired of hearing about it.

We get to Dallas and they were right. It was hot as balls. I remember being on the field before the game and they have that little thermometer there and it's 100 and something and it felt even hotter than that.

I'm looking at this psychological game that's being played. It's before the game and we're in the locker room and everyone is saying how hot is and all this other stuff. And I'm like, "Fuck that." I don't care how hot it is. Now I'm going off. I'm saying we're going to go out there and kick their ass. And you ain't ready for this, da da da. I'm pissed, because we got these cats crying about the heat, crying about the Cowboys. I'm like, "Fuck the heat. Fuck the Cowboys." Everyone looked at me like I lost my mind. But I hadn't played in what seemed like forever. It's the start of a new season. I'm ready to go. And these motherfuckers are acting like they're scared. And this young-ass Corey Simon is talking shit to me. Fuck all of that.

The Eagles dismantled the Cowboys right from the start. Ironically they held the same 24–6 halftime lead they held a year earlier at home against the Cardinals. This time they didn't blow it. Instead they blew out the Cowboys, 41–14. They outgained the home team, 425–167, as Duce Staley ran for a career-high 201 yards and a touchdown. Donovan McNabb ran for one touchdown and threw for another. The defense recorded five sacks, two by Douglas and one from the rookie Simon. And linebacker Jeremiah Trotter had a pick-six. Douglas' pregame fervor got everyone ready to go, including the head coach.

We go out there and we start with an onside kick (recovered by another Douglas, wide receiver Dameane, who is no relation). Andy doesn't say a whole lot, but he had to hear me in the locker room and I think I got him pumped up, too. We start with that onside kick and we go out there and we just kick the Dallas Cowboys' ass.

Everyone called it the pickle-juice game because we drank pickle juice all week to stay hydrated. And what happened was our trainer Rick Burkholder got in trouble. Because Gatorade was the official sponsor (of the NFL) and they were mad because everyone called it the pickle-juice game. We did drink Gatorade too. But we drank a lot of pickle juice.

So after that game I had to say something before every game or Andy would get nervous. "Hugh, you're not talking, you okay? What's wrong?" But you know how we feel about Dallas. And we're riding to the game and we see all that Cowboys stuff. We had to kick their ass. You know how people talk about attitude and swagger? That team had at-ti-tude. So when I said we're going to kick their ass and all of that, everyone looked at me and said, "Yeah, we are." And we did.

There wasn't a lot of momentum from the Dallas win. The Eagles lost their next two games—their home opener against the Giants, 33–18, and an ugly game at Green Bay, 6–3. They then won four of their next five, with the only loss at home to Washington. Sitting at 5–4, they closed the season with wins in six of their final seven games. The first two were overtime wins over Dallas, 16–13 at home, and at Pittsburgh, 26–23. The only loss was a tough 15–13 decision to the Tennessee Titans. The win over the Steelers highlighted that at-ti-tude and was also sort of a coming-out party for quarterback Donovan McNabb.

Pittsburgh led 23–13 with 3:47 to play in the fourth quarter. The Eagles outscored the Steelers 13–0 the rest of the way, with the Pittsburgh offense never seeing the field again. McNabb engineered a touchdown drive by going 4-for-4 on the possession and connecting with running back Brian Mitchell for six with 2:29 to play. Down 23–20, the Eagles executed another perfect onside kick and McNabb completed four more passes to set up kicker David Akers, who had missed from 38 yards out earlier in the fourth, for a 42-yard field goal to tie the game with 0:01 on the clock. The Eagles won the overtime coin toss, took the ball, and McNabb went 3-for-3 to set up Akers from the same 42 yards out for the win.

I think we all started seeing it from Donovan that year. Funny thing, one of the first things I remember about "Five" (McNabb) is every Friday, Andy had a set up for us where we would get cheesesteaks, chicken wings, all that kind of stuff. It was just on Fridays. We would have it in the locker room at the old Vet (Veterans Stadium) and it was set up right in the middle of the room. So it's Friday and the caterer comes in with the food and here comes Donovan. He walks up to it with his jock strap on and starts eating. That was it. That's all he had on was his jock strap and some flip flops. I thought that was the funniest shit I'd ever seen. And he was a rookie. I was like, "This cat is different." He probably doesn't even remember it, but I'll never forget it. We started calling it Jocks and Wings after that. He actually walked up there with just a jock strap on, his ass hanging out. It was like, "What's wrong with you?" But he fit right in with us with all the shenanigans and other stuff we would do.

Donovan was a leader, but he was a different kind of leader. And you could tell right from the go he was confident, really confident.

That 15–13 loss to Tennessee was the only blemish throughout the months of November and December for the Eagles, who followed the overtime wins with a blowout of Arizona and a revenge win at Washington. The Tennessee loss, like so many that season, came down to the final seconds. In a defensive battle, in which Douglas recorded a sack of Steve McNair, the Eagles took a 13–12 lead on a two-yard run by McNabb with 3:11 left in the fourth quarter. Tennessee went three-and-out and punted. But the Eagles did the same. The Titans got the ball back with 1:46 to play and …

McNair took them right down the field. I remember that game well. Because I was talking shit to (Tennessee left tackle) Brad Hopkins all game. And Brad Hopkins kicked my ass all the way down the field on that last drive. That was one time me talking shit backfired.

McNair completed six passes on that final drive and age-old Al Del Greco kicked a 50-yard field goal with five seconds on the clock to give the Titans the win. The Eagles came back and won their final two games of the regular season against the Cleveland Browns, 35–24, and the Cincinnati Bengals, 16–7. That left them at 11–5, good for the fourth seed in the six-team NFC playoffs and earning them home field for the wild-card game against the Tampa Bay Buccaneers to start the playoffs.

It was a long time coming. We hadn't had a playoff game at home in a while. I think Ray's first year (1995 against Detroit). The Vet (Veterans Stadium) was rocking like I had never seen it before. It was exciting. It was exciting to see the city rocking like that. It was just a great feeling.

On a chilly day in Philadelphia where the temperature was just above freezing but high winds made it a feel a lot colder, the Eagles dominated the team from Florida. After a slow start—the first quarter ended 0–0—the Eagles took over on both sides of the ball and breezed to a 21–3 win over Tony Dungy's Buccaneers. McNabb again was the key on offense, with touchdown passes to tight end Jeff Thomason and wide receiver Na Brown and a five-yard touchdown run of his own. Douglas led a defense that held Tampa to 199 total yards, with two of the team's four sacks of Tampa Bay quarterback Shaun King. Douglas' friend Hollis Thomas and his draft-mate Mike Mamula combined for the other two sacks. With Tampa ahead 3–0 early in the second quarter, Douglas sacked King, forced the ball loose, and Mamula recovered the fumble at the Tampa 15-yard line. McNabb ran for 10 yards to the 5. And on third-and-goal from the 5, ran for the touchdown and a 7–3 lead the Eagles would never relinquish.

I remember on that sack of Shaun King, they had (running back) Warrick Dunn in the backfield trying to block. Yeah, it turned out to be a big play in the game.

Dunn, the Bucs' leading rusher, not only got run over for the key sack, Douglas threw him for a loss on one of his eight runs. Douglas wasn't alone in that regard, however. Dunn's eight carries on the day netted a total of one yard.

The defense was ready. Everyone was making plays. Mike, Hollis, Troy (Vincent) and Bobby (Taylor) broke up some passes. It was just an overall team effort. We came ready to play.

It was the first of five straight playoff appearances for the Eagles, who would go to the postseason eight times between 2000 and 2010.

As a player you go through stages. You go to college and you aspire to be a NFL player. You get to the NFL and you make a whole lot of money. Now you have money, so then what? You want to be remembered. You want to be immortal. The only way to do that is to go to the Hall of Fame or win a Super Bowl. I aspired to go to the Hall of Fame, I'm not going to lie. I didn't do that. But I did get to a Super Bowl. So making the playoffs, for me that was the start.

That first playoff run ended the following week when for the third time that season the Eagles lost to their NFC East rival, the New York Giants. Ron

Dixon returned the opening kickoff 97 yards for a 7–0 lead and the Giants coasted to a 20–10 win that wasn't that close. It was 20–3 before McNabb connected with Torrance Small for a touchdown pass with 1:56 left in the game. The Giants defense held the Eagles to 186 total yards, sacked McNabb six times, and forced three turnovers. One of those turnovers was an incredible interception by Jason Sehorn that the Giants cornerback returned 32 yards for a touchdown and a 17–0 lead. Sehorn's pick six was voted by Giants fans as the greatest play in Giants Stadium history.

Yeah the Giants, that was the third time they beat us that year. They were good, really good. Then they went to the Super Bowl and got trounced by Baltimore.

While the Eagles season ended that day at the Meadowlands, Douglas had one more game to play—the Pro Bowl in Honolulu. It would be the first of three trips he would make to play in the NFL's All-Star Game. And he went and played in all three, never turning down the chance or opting out as several players have done over the years.

Making the Pro Bowl, that was great. It felt like back when I played—damn it feels funny to say that—but making the Pro Bowl meant you were with the elite. You were considered the best of the best. Only three defensive ends were picked to go and I was one of them. (Washington's Marco Coleman and New Orleans' Joe Johnson were the other two in 2000.) To be there with those guys, guys you've heard about and played against, that was a great feeling, a hell of a feeling. I loved it.

Douglas was one of five Eagles to make the trip to Hawaii that season. Cornerback Troy Vincent, linebacker Jeremiah Trotter, and tight end Chad Lewis were all voted into the game. And quarterback Donovan McNabb was added as an injury replacement.

Hawaii was cool. The place where we stayed was beautiful. It was a great experience. I had been to Hawaii before, because I played in the Hula Bowl in college. But it was the first time I went with some money in my pocket.

CHAPTER 10
52 YARDS AWAY

It felt like it was time. It just felt like it was our year. You get a taste of the playoffs, and think about it—a lot of us hadn't been to the playoffs. So to be in a position to be a good playoff team, that was a great feeling. It just felt like everything was coming together. The city was alive. We were winning. When I first got here we weren't doing a lot of winning, so it was tough to be in that situation. To finally be winning and have the city gravitate to us like that, it was awesome.

The 2001 Philadelphia Eagles, just a few years removed from the losingest season in team history, came within just over half a football field of going to the Super Bowl. They made it to the NFC Championship Game, where they lost to the St. Louis Rams, 29–24. Actually the 2001 Eagles season was symmetrical. They began and ended the season with losses to the Rams. The opener was an overtime loss and the NFC Championship Game came down to the final minutes. In between there were a lot of big wins and big plays, several of those plays from defensive end Hugh Douglas, who made it to his second consecutive Pro Bowl.

I remember being in the huddle a lot of times, and as I said I played with a great group of guys, but I would say, "Somebody has to make a play!" Now, I would freelance a lot. So I would say to Hollis (defensive tackle Thomas), "Cover me." I thought they were going to throw the ball and I would run my own stunts sometimes. Hollis would cover me and we would have a great time. I would just turn to him and say, "Tank, cover me, I'm going in."

And he would say, "You got it."

There were times we were in the huddle and everyone is going over the play call and my mind would be somewhere else. I would be like, "Hey, look at the cheerleaders over there doing their thing." And Hollis would have to tell me the play over and over again. It was wild.

Douglas was again the catalyst up front for an Eagles defense that played out of its mind in 2001. Opposing offenses scored a total of 208 points in 16 games. That comes out to exactly 13 points per game. The most points they allowed in any one game was 29 and four times they held teams to 10 points or less. Defensive coordinator Jim Johnson's mantra was if the defense held the opposing offense to 17 points or less, the team should win. Well they held them to an average of 13 and the team won 11 times before the playoffs and cruised to their first division title since 1988.

We had a good defense, a real good defense. I was able to freelance and do my own thing, because of the other guys we had. We especially had the secondary, Troy (Vincent), Bobby (Taylor), Dawk (Brian Dawkins), Al (Harris), and D-Mo (Damon Moore), those guys brought it every game. They could play. Those guys back there, when I think back on it, I couldn't have played with a better group of guys in the secondary.

Troy was the guy. He was the leader. He always had a level head. Al wanted to get paid. He wanted that bread. He came from a small school, Texas A&M-Kingsville, a small school just like I did and Al was trying to maximize his dollars. He was a hell of a corner. Al could play. He wanted to get traded to be a starter. He hated that he was stuck behind Bobby and Troy. Then he finally did get traded, went to Green Bay and blew up. That was good for him.

Douglas led the Eagles defense with 9½ sacks in 2001. He had a clause in his contract that earned him a nice bonus for 10 sacks. When the team clinched the NFC East with a game remaining and a playoff game scheduled the next week against the same Tampa Bay team they finished the season against, it was a good idea to rest some of the starters. Unless you needed another half-sack for a bonus. Stories were written that tried to pressure the front office to give Douglas the bonus money since it was the team's decision to rest him. Of course team president Joe Banner did not budge.

I forget exactly how much the bonus was, but it was a few hundred thousand. I understood it. We were winning and getting ready to go to the playoffs. So it was, "Do I want the money or do I want to be ready for the playoffs?" And to the Eagles credit they moved it around, redid my deal, and I ended up getting the bonus. So they did me right.

You know, I had a better relationship with Joe after I left the Eagles than I ever did when I played there. I think that's true with everybody.

Joe's job was to be the bad guy and Joe was a great bad guy, a really great bad guy. That was his role. This was early into their football days for Joe and Jeffrey. The Jeffrey Lurie that owns the team (in the 2020s) is not the Jeffrey Lurie that was there at the beginning. They were still trying to figure it all out as far as the draft and making moves and all of that.

I will say this: I played for a few others and I've talked to players who played for other organizations, and the Eagles organization is hands down one of the better organizations from top to bottom. It's the small details. They take care of their players. From nutrition, exercise, everything is catered to make you an optimum athlete. The way they take care of the players from top to bottom is just first class. Take the weight room. I remember when the weight room was a small room outside of the locker room. And on top of that we practiced and played in the same locker room (at Veterans Stadium). It's phenomenal the way they evolved from where they were when I first got there. Now they have a separate facility (NovaCare Complex) for practice with a nice weight room and they play at the Linc (Lincoln Financial Field).

In 2001, coming off a playoff appearance in 2000 that ended with a loss to the New York Giants, the team began slowly. There was the tough overtime loss to the Rams, in which they came back from a 17–3 deficit to force the extra session, a one-point loss to the Cardinals, 21–20, and a 20–10 setback to their old offensive coordinator Jon Gruden and the Oakland Raiders. After six games the Eagles were just 3–3.

We needed to get going. We were better than that. We were too good to be a .500 team.

They did. The Eagles won six of their next seven games to pull away in the East and all six wins were by double digits. They pummeled the Minnesota Vikings, 48–17, and throttled the rival Dallas Cowboys, 36–3. There were also easy wins over the Kansas City Chiefs and San Diego Chargers and revenge wins over the Cardinals and Washington Redskins. Quarterback Donovan McNabb, in his second full season as the starter, established himself as the team leader and one of the better quarterbacks in the conference with his second trip to the Pro Bowl. This time he was voted in by the players and coaches, not as a replacement. Duce Staley led the team in rushing with 604 yards and also caught 63 passes for 626 yards. James Thrash was McNabb's favorite receiver with 833 yards. Douglas' 9½ sacks were tops, while his buddy Corey Simon finished with 7½. They were two of 15 players to have at least one sack. Eight different players had interceptions. Douglas and McNabb were joined by Vincent, Dawkins, linebacker Jeremiah Trotter, tight end Chad Lewis, left tackle Tra Thomas, and kicker David Akers on the NFC team in the Pro Bowl. With no other team in the division over .500 that year the Eagles clinched with a week to play and were headed to what they hoped were bigger and better things. It started again with Tampa Bay.

We shut them down pretty good if I remember.

The warm-weather Bucs couldn't use the weather as an excuse this year. It was a balmy 46 degrees in Philadelphia on this January day. And in a game that took less than three hours to play, the Eagles beat the Buccaneers, 31–9. McNabb threw touchdown passes to Staley and Lewis, while Correll Buckhalter had a 25-yard touchdown run. Douglas had the defense's only sack of Brad Johnson. And he was involved in holding Bucs running back Warrick Dunn to 29 yards on 11 carries. The secondary picked off Johnson four times, two by Moore, who ran one back 59 yards for a touchdown. Vincent and Dawkins had the other two picks.

Tampa was out of the way and now it was on to Chicago for the Bears. Back then two teams had byes and the Bears (the No. 2 seed) had a bye. So we had to go there. But we were ready.

In what was the last game played at old Soldier Field—they started deconstruction of the stadium just minutes after the game ended and us writers were still in the press box. With 13 minutes remaining in the second quarter and the Eagles leading 6–0, "The Play" happened. Moore got his third interception of the playoffs, this one off the Bears Jim Miller, and was bringing it back as he did a week before against Tampa Bay. The quarterback tried to get in the way.

It started before the game. There was some animosity between us and the Bears going into the game. The night before their fans were calling our rooms with "Da Bears" shit on the phone. They got our room numbers and were keeping us up all night calling and saying, "Da Bears." So we get to Solider Field the next day, and it's cold (19 degree wind chill), and I remember this like it was yesterday. I walk out with just my little Under Armour shirt on. The Bears wide receivers are going through their drills and Bobby Taylor goes over to their drills and starts slapping balls out of their hands. And he says, "Don't worry about that, you're not going to catch shit today."

I was like, "Okay, Bobby, that's what we're doing today. Okay then. That's what we're doing today."

Now we're kicking their ass. D Mo gets the interception and I see Jim Miller and I said, "Jim, don't move. If you move I'm going to fuck you up."

Jim is laughing. My job—and I can still hear Jim Johnson saying it: "If they throw an interception, somebody go get the quarterback because he's the last line of defense at that point. If he acts like he's going to the ball you take his ass out."

So I told Jim Miller, "Don't move." I guess he thought I was playing. My job is to make sure I know where he is—I don't know what's going on behind me, I don't know where the ball is. Now, he starts dancing around like the ball is coming his way. I pick him up and I dump him on his shoulder. He's on the ground and he's rolling around in pain. So now he's out of the game. The backup (Shane Matthews) comes in and he didn't want any part of us.

McNabb connected with fullback Cecil Martin for a 13-yard touchdown pass with 14 seconds left in the first half to give the Eagles a 13–7 lead. Martin, a 1999 sixth-round pick out of Wisconsin, was a good find for the Eagles. He played four solid years for them, taking over for Kevin Turner, who retired in 1999.

Cecil was a good dude. He was a little eccentric, but a good dude. He had some good games for us. He was the kind of guy who kept to himself mostly. He's been to a few alumni events in recent years, and it seems like he's doing pretty well for himself. That was early in Andy's tenure when the fullback still mattered. We had good fullbacks. Kevin Turner, God rest his soul, was there first and then I think Cecil came in for Kevin. It's amazing how that position just died out over the years. That's an old-school position. Now guys all just want to tote the rock.

After the Bears took a 14–13 lead, McNabb found Staley for a six-yard touchdown pass, Akers added two field goals and the lead was in double digits, on the way to a 33–19 Eagles victory.

But (Matthews) gets on the podium after the game and says it was a dirty play. So now I'm up on the podium. First thing I said was I must have done something good, because I'm up here. Then they tell me what he said about a dirty play. I said, "Kiss my ass, I told him not to move." (Matthews) would have got the same thing if he were out there. They didn't throw a flag on the play—although I did get fined later in the week. But I didn't care. If I had to do it again, I would do the same thing.

What I remember most about the Chicago game wasn't the game, or that Jim Miller hit, but that Troy got hurt. Talk about, oh shit, that changes everything.

Vincent suffered a groin injury in the second half of the win over the Bears. He was going to be day-to-day for the NFC Championship Game against the Rams the following Sunday in St. Louis.

When Troy got hurt I used to sit with him during his treatments, because I wanted him to get better. Troy had a groin pull, but it was so bad he was going to need surgery at the end of the year to put mesh in his groin or whatever. So every day I'm sitting there and I'm asking Rick (Burkholder, the team trainer), "Is he going to be all right? Is he going to be all right?" We needed him (against the Rams). We needed all our corners. That was "The Greatest Show on Turf." We were cool with Al. But we needed that third corner. To not have that third corner hurt, that really hurt.

Now it's the night before the game and I remember sitting with Troy that night. And I'm just hoping he can go. And he did. He played the first half and played his ass off. He played great that first half. Then he re-injured it and the wheels just fell off the wagon for us.

With Vincent on the field, the Eagles led the Rams, 17–13, at the half. Staley had a one-yard touchdown run that evened the score, 10–10, and after the Rams took a 13–10 lead, McNabb hooked up with Todd Pinkston for a 12-yard touchdown with 46 seconds left in the half.

First let me say that was the absolute loudest building I've ever been in or played in my whole career. Those fans were loud.

That first half we shut them down. We were on (Rams quarterback) Kurt Warner's ass. We were pressuring him a lot. But when Troy got hurt, that was it. All I remember after that was the back of Marshall Faulk's jersey. They gave Marshall Faulk the ball and all I saw was the back of his jersey the rest of the day. He really was all that. We did a good job on him the first half. But when Troy got hurt it just changed everything. I'm convinced if Troy didn't get hurt we would have won that game and we would have beaten the Patriots (in the Super Bowl), too.

The Rams scored the first 16 points of the second half to take a 29–17 lead with 6:55 to play. Faulk, who scored two touchdowns, finished with 159 yards on 31 carries. Still, the Eagles had a chance. McNabb scored on a three-yard run with 2:56 left to make it a one-score game. The defense forced the Rams into a three-and-out and the offense got the ball back, after a 16-yard punt return by Brian Mitchell, at their 45-yard line with 2:20 on the clock.

McNabb completed a pass to rookie wide receiver Freddie Mitchell, but it went for just two yards. Staley managed just a yard on second-and-8. On third-and-7 from the 48-yard line, McNabb threw incomplete for Mitchell and on fourth down went to the rookie again and this time it was picked off by Aeneas Williams.

I was sick. We were all sick. Hey, we were close and we knew it. We just had to gear up for the next year. And the goal was to get home-field advantage so we won't have to go on the road and play in a place like that dome.

CHAPTER 11

TAMPA BAY, NO WAY

We were so confident we were going to the Super Bowl we were trying to figure out how we could rent Rolls Royces and Bentleys, because the game was in San Diego. That's how confident we were that we were going to the Super Bowl. We had beaten them before. And it was going to be cold and they were coming to our place. We thought for sure we had this.

The Philadelphia Eagles 2002 season, while one of the most accomplished in the organization's history, ended the same way as the 2001 season did—with a loss in the NFC Championship Game. This one, however, wasn't on the road in the you-can't-hear-yourself-think Edward Jones Dome against the Rams and The Greatest Show on Turf. No, this was at home at Veterans Stadium in the cold to the can't-win-in-the-cold Tampa Bay Buccaneers. And it wasn't even that close, the Bucs won going away, 27–10.

It was terrible, just terrible. That one hurt. That was the absolute worst loss I've ever been a part of in my career. We had to watch them celebrate on our field. That was bad, real bad. And then to see them go and drag Oakland the way they did in the Super Bowl, man it was tough.

More on that loss and what the Bucs, and the Eagles, did to make Hugh Douglas a non-factor in the game later. First let's look at how the Eagles got back to the NFC title game for the second consecutive season and why they were favored to get to their first Super Bowl since 1980. Duce Staley led the offense that season with 1,029 yards rushing and 51 receptions for another 511 yards. Douglas led the defense with 12½ sacks and 20 tackles for a loss on the way to his third consecutive Pro Bowl. He would be joined in Hawaii by teammates Donovan McNabb, Chad Lewis, Troy Vincent, Brian Dawkins, Bobby Taylor, and David Akers.

We were good, real good. We wanted home field, after losing in St. Louis the year before, and we got it. It wasn't an easy year by any stretch, because we had to overcome a lot (losing quarterback Donovan McNabb for the last six games of the regular season, for one), but the defense especially really stepped up when it counted. We felt we could beat anybody.

The season began like it had for three of the first four years of the Andy Reid Era with an opening-day loss. This time it was to former Eagles defensive coordinator Jeff Fisher's Tennessee Titans, 27–24, in Nashville. Again, the Eagles led 24–10 at the half thanks to three McNabb touchdown passes to James Thrash, Duce Staley, and Chad Lewis. But the Eagles' offense, which allowed six sacks in the game, went nowhere in the second half. McNabb threw two interceptions and fumbled once and the Titans and Steve McNair fought back. Hugh Douglas had the only sack of McNair and also had two tackles for a loss.

It's kind of the way we practiced. We started slow and always got better as the season progressed. I remember Dawk pointed that out to me once. He said, "Historically, we always started slow." But the way we practiced and the way we did things, we got better as the year went on, so I think that's a testament to it. We started slow and just got better and better.

The Eagles started out in a pattern that 2002 season. They lost to the Titans, then won three straight. They lost at Jacksonville, then won three straight. They lost to the Colts, at home—it must have been something about the AFC South—and then won six straight to win the NFC East by two games over the wild-card–bound New York Giants. When the Eagles didn't lose they not just won, they blew out the opposition. There were 30-point wins over NFC East rivals Dallas and Washington, and double-digit wins over Houston, Tampa Bay, the New York Giants, and Arizona.

I remember those losses. Jacksonville, it was really hot and really humid. That's the game Five (McNabb) threw up. It was just so hot down there that day. And Indianapolis, Peyton Manning just blew us up that game.

One week after the loss to Manning and the Colts, the season hung in the balance. The Eagles beat the Cardinals, 38–14, to move to 7–3 on the season. In that game, however, McNabb suffered a broken ankle. If the team was going to get back to the playoffs, win the division, and secure that much-wanted home-field advantage, they were going to have to do it with a backup quarterback—or two.

The way I remember it was, when Don got hurt it was like, "Okay, we got Koy (Detmer). He's not Don, but he's been here. We'll be all right. We'll get by." Then Koy got hurt and it was A.J. (Feeley). We didn't know that much about A.J.

Detmer, the team's backup and younger brother of former Eagles quarterback Ty, got the start in Week 12 on Monday Night Football *against the soon-to-be NFC West champion 49ers in San Francisco. Both teams came into the game 7–3, but the Eagles got to eight wins after a 38–17 drubbing. Detmer was brilliant in the start. He completed 18 of his 26 passes for 227 yards and threw touchdown passes to Todd Pinkston for 25 yards and to Antonio Freeman for 11 yards. He also scored on a one-yard quarterback sneak to give the Eagles a 28–10 lead late in the third quarter. The 49ers didn't know what hit them. And then Detmer wasn't sure what hit him. He went out with an elbow injury in the second half that ended his season.*

We were in the locker room and Joe Banner came in and he was having a fit. I mean, we were one of the picks to go to the Super Bowl that year. People were picking us to go to the Super Bowl and win the Super Bowl. And he was talking to Andy and I overheard the conversation. Everyone is shitting bricks because now Koy's hurt and they don't know what A.J. is going to bring to the table. And I'm hearing this and I got pissed. We're still here. We still got a good defense. We just have to play a little harder. I'm looking at Joe and I'm like, "We're here. We'll be all right until Donovan gets back." And that was the attitude we took. We knew Donovan was special, but we knew we had to hold the fort down until he came back. That was just the reality of the situation. Hold down the fort until Don gets back.

Did we know he was coming back? We thought he was. I mean, he played that last game with the broken ankle (and threw four touchdown passes in the win over the Cardinals). So it was like okay, "Just hold the fort until the Big Dog gets back." We just have to tighten our belts. We knew what Don meant to the offense and without him we were probably mediocre at best. Because Don was more than just a good quarterback.

His running ability gave us a whole different dynamic. He would freeze the secondary, because of his ability to run the ball, and he could throw it deep, too. So with him gone and now Koy gone as well, it was up to the defense. And that was the attitude on defense, just hold the fort.

Feeley, in his second year after being a fifth-round draft pick out of Oregon in 2001, had thrown all of 14 passes (he completed 10) as a rookie before being called on to finish the 49ers game and then more importantly finish the season.

We just told A.J., "Go play your game, we got you." If he didn't make mistakes, we'll find a way to win the game. That was our message. Just don't put us in a bad spot. And for the most part he did that. He did what he was supposed to do and the defense did the rest.

Feeley won his first four starts. The defense held both the Rams and the Cowboys to just three points and the team also had its way in wins over Seattle and Washington. The quarterback's numbers in those four wins were a modest 70-for-126 for 844 yards with five touchdowns and four interceptions. He was only sacked six times in the four games. And the most important stat was the Eagles were 12–3 after those four games.

It worked out great for A.J. He went to Miami (in a trade for a draft pick before the 2004 season), made some money, and married (soccer star) Heather Mitts. It worked out really great for him.

Feeley and the Eagles, on a cold and dreary Saturday afternoon, lost the final regular season game of 2002 at the Meadowlands to the Giants, 10–7, in overtime. The playoffs and the NFC East were already clinched before the game began. Home-field advantage was not. But when the Green Bay Packers lost to the New York Jets the next day it meant the Eagles, Packers, and Bucs all finished 12–4. Those early losses to the AFC South turned out to be important, because the Eagles won the tiebreaker over both Green Bay and Tampa Bay, thanks to an 11–1 record in the NFC.

We wanted home field and we got it.

That meant a first-round bye and then a date with Michael Vick and the Atlanta Falcons, who a week earlier became the first team to ever win a playoff game against the Green Bay Packers at Lambeau Field. The Packers, coached at the time by Mike Sherman, could not contain the mercurial Vick. So after all those years, Atlanta finally got even with Sherman.

We knew Michael Vick was more of a threat out of the pocket than he was throwing it from the pocket. So Jim (defensive coordinator Johnson) was like, "Listen, let's keep him in the pocket." And we did a lot to confuse him with our different looks. Our whole plan was to just make sure Vick doesn't get loose. Don't let him out of the pocket. And then we wanted to flush him to the left. He beat Green Bay the week before by running. He ran all over the place. They couldn't stop him. We didn't let him run.

That Eagles defense that led the team to the playoffs and the first-round bye, actually outscored the Atlanta offense in the 20–6 win. Bobby Taylor picked off a Vick pass in the first quarter and returned it 39 yards for a touchdown and a 7–0 lead. Vick ran the ball just six times for 30 yards. McNabb, in his first game back since he broke his ankle seven week earlier, completed 20 of 30 passes for 247 yards and a touchdown pass to James Thrash. Duce Staley ran for 65 yards and caught five passes for 39 yards. Now it was back to the NFC Championship Game against Tampa Bay. The third straight year they would meet the Bucs in the playoffs. Only this time the Tampa head coach was Jon Gruden, not Tony Dungy. So it didn't matter all that much that the game-time temperature was 26 degrees with a wind chill factor of 16 degrees.

Tampa Bay had a good game plan. When Jon Gruden was doing *Monday Night Football* on ESPN I saw him and he told me—and I hated hearing this—but he told me, "We couldn't block you. We had a game plan where we weren't going to let you on the field. We knew when we went to a certain front you were off the field." So they played that front all game basically. It was a run formation front and I came off the field on run formations. Every time they got into this formation, I would come off the field. But they would pass out of that formation.

I remember I kept saying, "Jim, I'll play the run. I just want to win the game." They were gassing us. And I'm standing on the sideline. I hated it. But it was a formation I wasn't familiar with so Jim didn't want to put me out there. My thing was, if they ran the ball, so what? I didn't give a shit at that point. The percentage was they were passing out of that formation. They were doing it all day. But Jim didn't want to change the game plan. I didn't play a lot of snaps that game. And I was hot. I kept saying, "I'll do whatever I have to do." But it wasn't our game plan and I understood, but it wasn't a good feeling. It wasn't a good feeling at all.

With Brandon Whiting and ND Kalu on the field at defensive end more than Douglas, journeyman Bucs quarterback Brad Johnson competed 20 of 33 passes for 259 yards. He threw a touchdown pass to Keyshawn Johnson that broke a 10–10 tie and gave the Bucs the lead for good. And he connected with Joe Jurevicius for a 71-yard catch and run on third-an-2 from the Bucs 24-yard line that made it first-and-goal from the 5-yard line. The Bucs running game managed just 49 yards on 32 carries, but included a touchdown run from fullback Mike Alstott.

That Jurevicius play, (safety) Blaine Bishop was playing with a bad groin, or something, and was chasing him the whole way.

When Brian Mitchell returned the opening kickoff 70 yards to the Tampa 30-yard line and Staley scored on a 20-yard run two plays later, it was 7–0, because of history and 26-degree weather it felt as if the game was over. I actually turned to the writer next to me in the press box and said, "It's going to be a blowout." I was right. It was just the wrong team doing the blowing.

We had the kickoff return and bang we're up 7–0. Then all of a sudden it switched. All the momentum switched. And they went to that Elephant Package and I was on the sideline.

While Gruden's offensive game plan worked just as he drew it up during the week. Andy Reid's pass-happy offense did not go as the coach saw it at practice on Wednesday and Thursday. After Staley's 20-yard touchdown run, he got just 12 carries the rest of the game. McNabb, in his second game back, threw the ball 49 times. His 43rd pass, with the Eagles down 20–10 with 3:27 left in the game, was intercepted by Ronde Barber and returned 92 yards for a game-sealing touchdown. Earlier in the week veteran running back Dorsey Levens joked that, "The only time Andy runs the ball is to give the wide receivers a break." Maybe he wasn't joking.

It was bad. It was real bad.

What made it worse was it was the Eagles' last game at Veterans Stadium. The multi-purpose venue in South Philadelphia had hosted the Eagles and the Phillies since 1971, but was being knocked down and replaced by a football-only stadium, Lincoln Financial Field, and a baseball-only stadium, Citizen's Bank Park. There may not have been another place in the NFL that opposing teams dreaded more than "The Vet" and it ended with 65,000-plus fans leaving it as they would a funeral, somber, tearful, and knowing they would never see this place again. Or if they would ever see the Eagles get past an NFC title game.

The Vet was a shithole. But it was our shithole. It was old and it was nasty. It was disgusting. And we did everything there, practiced, played, everything. People hated playing at The Vet. They hated it. But it was home to us. You would see teams come in and then the psychological advantage for us. You would see their running backs, their wide receivers, walk around and say, "Look at this, look at that."

We would see that and say, "We got this one."

They would always ask us, "How do you guys play on this? It's like cement."

And we'd be like, "Yeah, but it's home." It was bad. My knees and back still hurt from playing there. But it was home. It was home to all of us.

While the loss to Tampa Bay ended the Eagles season one game short of the Super Bowl and sent The Vet out on a sour note, it also ended another era. Or at least that was the feeling that night.

That loss hurt, it really hurt. We were so close (to the Super Bowl) and we thought this was the year. And for me personally it really hurt even more, because I felt it was probably going to be my last game as an Eagle.

CHAPTER 12
FREE AGENCY

Yeah, it hurt. It hurt a lot. And here's the irony, right after I agreed to sign the deal with Jacksonville, that's when I heard from Jeffrey Lurie. It was too late at that point. I already gave my word to the Jaguars.

Hugh Douglas, despite playing and not practicing with a bad knee for the second half of the 2002 season, was still one of the Eagles best defensive players that year and was selected to his third consecutive Pro Bowl. He easily led the team in sacks with 12½. N.D. Kalu was second with eight. He led the team—and the NFL—in tackles for a loss with 20. Darwin Walker and his old buddy Corey Simon were second with 11. And he led all of the team's defensive linemen in tackles with 53. Brandon Whiting and Simon were second with 39. All of those numbers were not as important to team president and financial negotiator Joe Banner than 32. That's how old Douglas would be at the start of the 2003 season. And the Eagles, under Banner, did not give long-term deals to players over 30. They just didn't.

I didn't know what was going to happen (in free agency). I was coming off a good year, but I hadn't heard anything (from the Eagles). And remember the year before they let Trot (Jeremiah Trotter) go. Now it was my turn. And it wasn't looking good. It wasn't looking good for me at all as far as staying with the Eagles. They didn't talk to anybody, me or my agent. From what I recall, it was kind of like: see what you can get. That was the feel I got from Drew (agent Rosenhaus). Go around and see what you're worth.

Most players embrace free agency. They can't wait to become one. Because for the first time in their careers they get to make the choice of where they want to play. Hell, it's what the players went on strike for in 1987, to get the right to have unrestricted free agency. For Douglas, who was drafted by the New York Jets, a team he almost said no to because he hoped to get drafted a few picks later by the Detroit Lions, and was then traded to the Philadelphia Eagles, another place he did not want to go, this should have been great—the climax of his brilliant career. It wasn't. He ended up going somewhere he really didn't want to go, since he really didn't want to go anywhere.

It was weird. My son (Hugh Jr.) was just born and I didn't know what the next phase of my life was going to be. I just didn't know. So it was a strange situation for me. I enjoyed going to see other teams and other places, but I never really wanted to leave Philadelphia. But I figured out that that was not going to be the case. I probably wasn't going to go back. So it was only a matter of time.

Douglas made three free agent visits during the offseason of 2003. He went to Seattle, to Kansas City, and just up the New Jersey Turnpike to the New York Giants.

It was funny. When I was in Seattle talking to the Seahawks, (head coach and general manager) Mike Holmgren was great. He was telling me how they were going to use me and how he told Andy (Reid, who was Holmgren's protégé when they were in Green Bay together) how much he wanted me. Seattle was on the cusp of being a good team. They weren't quite there yet, but they were getting there. But I remember flying out there and how far it was from home. I remember that more than anything. And after I left there I got a call from (Denver's Hall of Fame tight end) Shannon Sharpe. Shannon said, "Man, if you go to Seattle, you'll never be heard from again." That kind of stuck with me. Hugh Jr. was just born. (The family) would go out there with me. But that was just a long, long way from home. That was the biggest deterrent for me to go to Seattle.

Holmgren's Seahawks were coming off a 7–9 season in 2002, but made the playoffs in 2003, 2004, and went to the Super Bowl in 2005. But in Douglas' mind, location was more of a factor than the team's rising success at that point.

The Giants were never really a possibility. I just went there for the free meal. I actually went there because I was a big fan of Michael Strahan and we talked about it and everything. But what was funny was I didn't even pass their physical because of my knee. But I definitely wasn't going back to New York.

Kansas City, I loved talking to coach (Dick) Vermeil. They made me feel real comfortable and Coach Vermeil gave me the plan. We know you have a knee injury—remember I didn't practice the end of that last year—and Vermeil was like, we'll take care of you and this, that, and the third. But the money wasn't really what I wanted. My dumb ass, I wanted the money up front. I wanted it in one shot. Kansas City wanted to spread it out over the year. I wanted it in a signing bonus. I wanted the guaranteed money. Now looking back that's where I should have signed, Kansas City.

While Douglas and his agent thought it over and mulled over the distance to Seattle and the Chiefs offer, another call led to another offer and all of a sudden the pass-rushing defensive end was staying very close to his home in Atlanta and getting the money he wanted and when he wanted it.

At the last minute, Jacksonville came in and they gave me the money, the guaranteed money that I wanted. Jack (Jaguars head coach Del Rio) was all like, "We'll take care of you, yada, yada, yada," and all of that stuff. I never visited there. They just called us. They came in at the last minute and gave me what I wanted. The deal was done. Drew wanted to get me the best deal. And that's his job. He was trying to get the best deal for his client and Jacksonville was the best deal. That's what I was looking at, instead of looking at everything else, I was just focused on the money.

Jacksonville signed Douglas to a five-year, $27 million deal ($5.4 million average per year) with $6 million guaranteed in the signing bonus. By today's standards that's not much for a player who routinely puts up a double-digit sack numbers, but in 2003 it was pretty good.

If I had to do it all over again I wouldn't have changed a whole lot because of my situation. I knew this was probably going to be my last go-round. And I never heard from the Eagles, so this was it.

Again, he never heard from the Eagles until it was too late. That was the team's M.O. in those years. Players over 30 were shown the door and replaced by draft picks. The team, or at least the defense, that Ray Rhodes had put together in the late '90s was being taken apart piece by piece. Mike Mamula retired after the 2000 season. Trotter was let go—after the team pulled the franchise tag from him—in 2002 and landed in Washington. Douglas was allowed to leave for Jacksonville in 2003, the same year the team traded Al Harris to the Green Bay Packers. Troy Vincent and Bobby Taylor would play their last games as Eagles in 2003. Vincent signed as a free agent with Buffalo and Taylor with Seattle. Dawkins, the Hall of Fame safety, somehow lasted until 2008 before leaving for Denver.

It was just the way the team did business. The Eagles had already drafted cornerbacks Lito Sheppard and Sheldon Brown to replace Vincent and Taylor and drafted Jerome McDougle, out of Miami, in the first round of the 2003 Draft to replace Douglas. Ironically, and unfortunately for the Eagles, McDougle played just three years and had a total of three sacks in those three years. That was a good game for Douglas.

That was the Eagles plan to draft well and let the young guys take over.

Sometimes it worked, as with Sheppard and Brown, and sometimes it didn't (see McDougle). But it wasn't a coincidence that when tight end Brent Celek retired in 2017 he became the first Eagles player to play at least 10 years in the league all with them since tackle Jerry Sisemore, who retired in 1984. Under the new Eagles regime that's no longer the case.

I look at some players today like (former Eagles) Brandon Graham (who retired and unretired in 2025) and Jason Kelce (who retired in 2024) and I'm happy that they were able to play their whole career with one team. I wish I was able to stay in Philly but it wasn't meant to be. But it's great for them. You know how rare it is for a player to stay in one place his whole career. There just aren't that many who are able to do that. I mean, Brian Dawkins didn't even do it.

So I was headed off to Jacksonville.

CHAPTER 13
JACKSONVILLE

It was worse than my last year with the Jets. It really was. I wasn't happy with the city. I wasn't happy with the way they did things. I wasn't happy being the scapegoat. I'm not going to lie. I didn't like Jacksonville. I missed Philly.

Hugh Douglas spent just one year of his five-year deal with the Jacksonville Jaguars. What seemed like a good idea—close to home, defensive oriented head coach, good money—went wrong in a hurry. Well, the money was still good. It was just everything else.

You know shit started changing right away. Jack (head coach Del Rio) started acting weird. They knew I was hurt, right? Everyone knew I was hurt. And he never gave me the opportunity to get healthy. I remember he called me in one day and said, "You have to be out there at practice."

I told him, "You know I'm not healthy."

He said, "Yeah, but we need to have you out there. You need to be out there." So I'm out there doing the best I can, not knowing the whole time I'm being evaluated. They signed me and they knew I had a bone bruise on my knee. They knew that. Man, it became something totally different. It became I'm not healthy and I'm being critiqued.

Despite his defensive background and the fact he was a former player, Del Rio and Douglas rarely saw things the same way. Del Rio, almost at every turn, found something to criticize Douglas. This was not a happy marriage from the start.

And then this happened. He was like, you're a little heavy I need you to come in at this weight. And I was like, you knew I was hurt when you signed me. What the hell are you doing? But I didn't say anything. I just sucked it up. But everyone knew I was hurt when I signed. Everyone. I mean, they had my medicals. They were pressing me to practice. So I went out there and practiced. Now I'm trying to get healthy and I am doing what he's asking me to do. And it's just not working. It took me forever to get healthy. I had all kinds of issues with the knee hurting.

If the injury wasn't enough. The Jaguars defensive style didn't fit what Douglas had done his entire career and what he thought they paid him to do.

Then it was, they don't like my style of play. I mean, they watched me play before I signed, right? But it was more of them trying to get me to fit what they wanted me to do, instead of letting me do what they saw me do before they signed me. They ran a defense where they ran up the field to set the edge. I was a physical player. I played physical. They didn't like that or they didn't want that. They wanted the defensive ends to run up the field and set the edge. That's not what I did. I didn't understand it. I never did.

Jacksonville hired Del Rio as their head coach in 2003 after just one year as the Carolina Panthers defensive coordinator in 2002. A third-round pick by the New Orleans Saints, out of Southern Cal in 1985, he enjoyed an 11-year NFL career as a linebacker with the Saints, Kansas City Chiefs, Dallas Cowboys, and Minnesota Vikings. His best season was his next-to-last when he went to his lone Pro Bowl as a Viking. Ironically, Del Rio's last season as a player was 1995, the same year Hugh Douglas was winning the Defensive Rookie of the Year Award as a Jet. Del Rio's coaching career began in 1997 as the strength coach back in New Orleans with the Saints. After two seasons in New Orleans he became the Baltimore Ravens linebacker coach for three seasons and then the Panthers coordinator for one. Jacksonville hired the then 40-year-old Del Rio to replace Tom Coughlin as their head coach. He spent nine years with the Jaguars, made two playoff appearances, and had an overall record of 68–71. After being fired by Jacksonville he went to Denver as defensive coordinator before resurfacing in 2015 as head coach of the Oakland Raiders. In three years with the Raiders he made one playoff appearance and had a record of 25–23.

You could kind of tell it was his first year. Let me tell you what Jack did that year. He put a log in the locker room. And he tells us every day, "I want you to come in here and chop a piece of this wood because that's how we're going to be working." I'm not a fucking lumberjack. I'm not chopping shit. So these guys would come in every day and fuck around with that piece of wood and one day the kicker comes in and almost cuts off his leg. I'm telling you he damn near cut his leg off.

It got worse before it got better, because it never really got better for Douglas or the Jaguars in 2003.

First game there I had a sack (in a one-point loss to Carolina) but they didn't like the way I played. The coaches told me I have to do what they asked me to do. I'm like, shit this is how I've played my whole career. I played a physical game. So I tried to play it their way and I wasn't producing. Tony Brackens (a second-round pick of the Jaguars in 1996 who spent his entire eight-year career in Jacksonville, the final year in 2003) was the other defensive end and we weren't doing what they wanted us to do. It was a real clusterfuck.

Jacksonville lost its opener to Del Rio's former team, the Panthers, 24–23, and then lost three more to Buffalo, Indianapolis, and Houston to start the season 0–4. Del Rio's first win came at home against the San Diego Chargers, but then three more losses left them at 1–7 at the halfway point of the season. The Jaguars played .500 ball the second half, went 4–4, and finished 5–11 and tied for last in the AFC South. There was plenty of blame to go around, but a lot of it fell on the free agent the team spent $27 million on in the offseason.

Douglas, playing with a sore knee and in a defense that didn't fit his style, still played and started all 16 games. He recorded career lows in tackles (27), tackles for a loss (five), and sacks (3½). To this day, Jaguars fans hold him in disregard as one of the team's worst free agent signings. Hugh was right. He obviously signed with the wrong team.

I was the scapegoat. They killed me. But I never said anything. Nobody knew that when I signed there I was told I was going to be allowed to get healthy. And they didn't do that. There was nothing I could say to make anyone believe that. Jack held all the cards. And he would do stuff at practice to undermine me. What could I do? Years later, I saw Jack when I was working at ESPN. He said to me, "You didn't believe in what I was doing."

I said, "No, I didn't." We were cool, but he was just all over the place. He knew I was hurt, but he didn't care.

And I don't give a flying fuck what Jacksonville fans say about me. Because I know I wasn't healthy. The point was, I couldn't say anything because nobody would believe me. Dick Vermeil and Mike Holmgren, they knew and they were going to let me get healthy. Jack wouldn't do that. Like I said before, I should have gone to Kansas City.

While Douglas and the 2003 Jaguars struggled, his old team followed the same script as it had in 2001 and 2002. The Eagles started slowly, rallied, and won the NFC East, clinched home-field advantage in the playoffs, and then lost in the NFC Championship Game. This time it was to the Carolina Panthers, the team Del Rio left as defensive coordinator to become head coach of the Jaguars.

I didn't keep in touch with a lot of the guys in Philly because I knew they were playing and heading to the playoffs and didn't want to bother them. We did play Washington in the preseason and I saw Trot (Jeremiah Trotter) before the game. We hugged like we were two lost lovers who hadn't seen each other in ages. It was bananas. Even talking about it now I laugh. But as far as the Eagles, I would call Derek Boyko (the Eagles longtime public relations director) just to see what was happening there.

What happened was the Eagles lost their season opener—again. Jon Gruden's Tampa Bay Buccaneers, who beat them in the last game played at Veterans Stadium in the 2002 NFC Championship Game, beat them again on Monday Night Football *to open the team's brand-new Lincoln Financial Field. Eventual Super Bowl–champion New England beat the Eagles, 31–10, the following week to leave them at 0–2. They were 2–3 when one game, actually one play, saved their season.*

The Eagles trailed the New York Giants, 10–7, at the Meadowlands and were 1:34 away from falling to 2–4 on the season and 0–2 in the division (they lost to Dallas the week before). How bad were the Eagles that day? The offense gained a total of 134 yards and 89 of those yards came on the team's lone touchdown drive on its second possession of the game. The Eagles last six drives of the game totaled 15 yards. Quarterback Donovan McNabb was 9-for-23 for 64 yards, was sacked three times, and threw an interception. But the Eagles defense forced the Giants to punt on fourth-and-12 from the Eagles 46-yard line with that 1:34 on the clock. Former Eagles punter Jeff Feagles pooched one 30 yards, where it was fielded on the hop by Brian Westbrook at the 16. Eighty-four yards later the second-year back from Villanova was in the end zone and the Eagles had a 14–10 lead. The Giants had one last chance, but on fourth-and-4 from the Eagles 38-yard line, Bobby Taylor broke up a pass intended for tight end Jeremy Shockey.

We knew Brian was special, or was going to be special. We called him "The Boost." When I was there it was his rookie year and he wasn't playing a whole lot. He was mostly doing scout-team stuff. But you knew he was special because he didn't take any trash from us. And he worked his butt off every day at practice. I remember one day we're getting ready to play the Rams and Marshall Faulk. So Jim (defensive coordinator Johnson) would tell us every play to hit the running back. So we would do that to Brian. We're hitting him every play. Finally Brian says, "Fuck this shit, I'm not doing this anymore."

But he would crush us at practice. He would really give it to us. So Jim said that day, "Okay, hit him."

Yeah, we went a little overboard and Brian got tired of it and went off. We laughed and said, "Calm down, you're giving us a good look." But you could see he was going to be a really good back in the league. And he was. He was one of the best.

Westbrook's heroics against the Giants at the Meadowlands, the same Meadowlands where Herman Edwards scooped up a Joe Pisarcik fumble and returned it for a touchdown 25 years earlier in the first "Miracle," sparked the Eagles onto a nine-game win streak that got them to 11–3 on the season. An overtime loss to the San Francisco 49ers left them at 11–4 and a game behind the St. Louis Rams for the top seed in the NFC with a week to play. When the Eagles blew out Washington, 31–7, and the Rams lost to the Detroit Lions, 30–20, the Eagles moved past the Rams thanks to a better conference record. The Eagles first playoff game that year, after the first-round bye, was against the Green Bay Packers. There was a familiar face in the media for that one.

At the end of the year I was doing stuff for NFL Network. And one of the playoff games I did was the Eagles game against Green Bay. I remember showing up and it was like a homecoming for me, seeing all the guys. That was a great experience.

It took another miraculous finish from the most unlikeliest of sources for the Eagles to advance to their third consecutive NFC Championship Game. The Packers led most of the way and were ahead 17–14 as they attempted to run out the clock. Stopped on third-and-1 from the Eagles 40 with under two minutes to play, the Packers punted. The Eagles moved the ball early, but two incompletions and a sack set up fourth-and-26, you may have heard of that situation. McNabb dropped back and connected with wide receiver Freddie Mitchell over the middle for the first down. The Eagles would tie the game, 17–17, on a David Akers field goal. And win it overtime, 20–17, on another Akers field goal. It was Mitchell's play on fourth-and-26 that everyone remembers. The 2001 first-round draft pick had not done much up to that point except talk a good game. In his first two years he caught a total of 33 passes and in 2003 had just 35 receptions for 498 yards, not exactly first-round pick stuff. But as a talker, he was pure first round. He gave himself the nickname "Fred-Ex" because he always delivered. In one interview he thanked his hands for being so good. But Mitchell and McNabb just never hit it off, never seemed to get along on or off the field.

Yeah, Freddie's mouth was in a whole different stratosphere than his game. Freddie could play. But, for whatever reason, Freddie and Donovan's relationship just fizzled. Freddie was loud and boisterous and fun. But he would have been better if him and Donovan were better. You can't piss off the quarterback or you won't see the rock. Whatever happened between him and Donovan, it just didn't work out. And especially back then a wide receiver's success was hooked to his quarterback. If you don't have a good relationship, you have a problem. But Freddie could talk. He was pure comedy, man.

The Eagles overtime win sent them back to the NFC title game and a meeting with the third-seed Panthers, who upset the No. 2 seed Rams the week before. In this one, fourth-and-26 turned into third-and-none. McNabb, before injuring his ribs, was sacked four times and threw three interceptions. Backup Koy Detmer had one of each. With the score 7–3, Carolina running back DeShaun Foster scored on a one-yard touchdown run in which six Eagles defenders missed him.

I was sick at home for that game. I mean I was really sick. Sick as a dog.

And not because the Eagles lost to the Panthers.

No, I was rooting against them that day. I'll admit it. I was hating a little bit. I was like, "If these motherfuckers go to the Super Bowl without me, and I'm in Jacksonville, man I'm going to be mad." I'm watching the game at home and I'm thinking, "They're going to go without me."

They didn't. And a year later they did—with him.

CHAPTER 14
COMING HOME

We played a preseason game and one of the coaches said, "Hey, get a sack," or something like that. But I had a feeling that this might be it for me. I wanted it to be. Because I was just kind of fed up with the way things were going and everything else about that place.

Hugh Douglas was never meant to be a Jacksonville Jaguar and his days there were about to be over, much to his and head coach Jack Del Rio's delight. The only question was where would the pass-rushing defensive end go next to finish his brilliant career.

I remember going into the practice site and I had been drinking the night before so I was a little tipsy and I fell asleep on the training table. When I woke up the guys were like "(Del Rio) wants to see you."

I was like, "It took him long enough." I already knew what it was, what he was going to say.

So he walks me into his office and he was like, "Hey, man, I didn't want do this in front of everyone but I'm going to have to let you go."

And I was like, "No problem, no skin."

He kept talking and I was, "It's all good. Bye." When I left I didn't even clean out my locker. I just wanted to get out of there. It had gotten ridiculous. It was a shit show.

One of the first people Douglas reached out to was his old friend, Derek Boyko, the longtime Eagles public relations director, who is now with the Buffalo Bills. Would the Eagles be interested in a reunion? Boyko would know, or would find out.

I called Boyko and told him I just got cut. He was like, "You're kidding." I told him I wasn't sure what I was going to do, but I was going to do something. A few teams had called immediately when they heard I was cut. But I wanted to touch base with the Eagles.

Teams had to know if the knee that plagued Douglas throughout that 2003 season, the one the Jaguars wouldn't let get healthy, was going to be a factor.

It was better. I was better. It still wasn't 100 percent, but the knee was feeling better. Hey, I still wanted to play. I just didn't want to play for (the Jaguars). I was looking for one last bite of the apple.

Like I said, a few teams called. Then a good friend of mine, Bernard Johnson, heard I got cut and called me and said, "You better take your ass back to the Eagles." He said, "They're going to the Super Bowl. Go back to Philly. That's where you belong."

After I talked to Boyko, Andy (Reid) called and said, "What do you want to do?"

I said, "I'll come back." It wasn't for a whole lot of money, but it was being back in Philly. I came back and it was right before the last preseason game and I wanted to play. I remember I told Andy I wanted to play and he said no. I was just chomping at the bit. I wanted to show I could still play.

The Eagles team Douglas returned to for the 2004 season was not the team he left after the 2002 season. Both starting cornerbacks Troy Vincent and Bobby Taylor had left as free agents for Buffalo and Seattle respectively. The new corners were young players and high draft picks Lito Sheppard and Sheldon Brown, the team's first and third picks of the 2002 Draft. Safety Michael Lewis, drafted one spot before Brown, was starting at safety. Up front on defense, the team made a big free agent splash signing defensive end Jevon Kearse away from the Tennessee Titans, where he had set a rookie record with 14½ sacks in 1999. In his four healthy seasons with the Titans, Kearse had 45½ sacks. In his four seasons with the Eagles he had 22. The other defensive end was Derrick Burgess, a third-round pick out of Mississippi in 2001. When the team drafted him he was called "the next Hugh Douglas." Inside at defensive tackle, Douglas' friend Hollis Thomas was still there, but was a backup to Corey Simon and Darwin Walker, with youngster Sam Rayburn also getting snaps inside. The linebackers were also different. Dhani Jones came from the Giants to play the strong side and former Falcon Mark Simoneau was in the middle, at least to start the season. Jeremiah Trotter, like Douglas, had also returned. But he was a backup and special teams player when the season began.

It wasn't the same. I was spelling Derrick Burgess. D-Burg was out there doing his thing. I was just a backup. And that was cool. I didn't have a problem with that. I tried to make the most of it because I knew what the situation was at that point.

Burgess was Douglas' backup when he left and was somewhat of a mentor to him. Now, the younger player had gotten his opportunity and was not about to give it back.

No, it wasn't the same at all. It was different. But it was exciting. Dawk (Brian Dawkins) was still there and Trot was working his way back. Overall, it was somewhat of a younger squad. It was still like being at home, though. I enjoyed it. It was what I wanted at this stage. And when I came back I knew it was going to be different. We talked about that before I came back. My role was different. Derrick Burgess, I think initially he thought I was trying to take his job, which I was. But he was entrenched as the starter. I was just trying to fit in. He worked hard for it and waited his turn and it was his time. Whatever my role was I just wanted to show I could still play and help the team.

There was a new player on offense, a wide receiver named Terrell Owens, who the Eagles acquired in a roundabout way from the San Francisco 49ers via the Baltimore Ravens. On the same day the team signed and had a press conference for Kearse, it was announced the Ravens had acquired Owens from the 49ers. Television reports followed the Eagles brass—Reid, Joe Banner, and Jeffrey Lurie—on their way from their offices to the press conference. They were shocked. Why? They thought they were about to acquire Owens. It was a strange situation. Owens and his agent felt he had met clauses in his contract that made him an unrestricted free agent. The 49ers felt he had a year remaining on his deal and thus could trade him. The league got involved. Owens was declared somewhat of a free agent in that he got to go to the team of his choice, the Eagles. But the Eagles sent defensive end Brandon Whiting to the 49ers and a draft pick to the Ravens to seal the deal.

Listen, when I tell you T.O. was a huge difference maker it was undeniable. I mean, you couldn't deny it. We were a good team. And we had a lot of pull in the city, there's no question about that. But T.O. made it different. It was just different. It was like rock star status. He brought that to the team. T.O. brought a different feel to the Eagles. He brought a celebrity feel to the Eagles and he did it on a national level.

Owens made his mark on Philadelphia and Eagles fans right from the start of training camp, where over 20,000 of them packed Lehigh University every day and chanted his initials throughout the two-hour practices. It was unprecedented.

I remember seeing clips of that on television. It was crazy.

When the season started, T.O.-mania was at a fever pitch. He and Donovan McNabb looked like they were going to be the next great QB/WR duo in the league. In a season-opening 31–17 blowout of the rival Giants, McNabb threw for 330 yards and four touchdowns. Owens caught eight passes and three of the four touchdown passes. The always-slow-starting Eagles were off to a quick start in 2004. Except for Douglas. In his first game back in Philadelphia he got a sack of Hall of Fame quarterback Kurt Warner, but also suffered a torn rotator cuff.

I didn't play that final preseason game, but I played the opener against the Giants. We beat the brakes off the Giants but unfortunately for me I got hurt. In the first game. My first game back and I tore my arm, my rotator cuff. They told me I needed surgery. So I came back to Philly to miss the season and be on (injured reserve) for the season. Fuck that. This was probably my last go-round anyway, so I decided let's just ride it out and see what happens. I would have hated to be on IR all season and not contribute. I mean, the reason I came back was I wanted to play. And I knew this team could be special.

It was tough for me, real tough. I was a shell of myself. But there wasn't anything I could do about it, because that was the choice that I made. I didn't want to go on I.R. I wanted to play.

As Douglas tried to do what he could and not make the shoulder injury any worse than it was, he managed to play in all 16 regular-season games. The Eagles, specifically McNabb and Owens, continued to dominate the early part of the season. The team won its first five games all by double figures. Included in that was a 30–8 drubbing of the Carolina Panthers, the team that beat the Eagles in the NFC Championship Game the year before. Owens caught four passes for 123 yards in the win over Carolina. Imagine if he had gotten there a year earlier.

We started out a lot of games where we would just go deep. It was no more dink and dunk. We were going for the jugular. We played from ahead most games. We were taking tops off the defenses right from the start.

After the blowout of the Panthers, the Eagles had two tough ones—a 34–31 overtime win at Cleveland (McNabb threw for 376 yards and four touchdowns and Owens caught four passes for 109 yards and two touchdowns) and a 15–10 win over Baltimore at home.

That Baltimore game was tough. I remember T.O. ran a crossing route and Donovan was under pressure. Donovan had to throw it quickly and the ball damn near hit the ground. I remember this like it was yesterday. T.O. picked up that ball just off the ground like it was a baby. This ball was low, super low, I don't think anyone else could have caught it. T.O. catches it in stride and goes in for the touchdown. I said, "Oh shit, this team is special. That guy is special. We got a shot." It was just a different feel. Practice felt different. Everything was different.

The Steelers ended the Eagles' undefeated season with a 27–3 rout in Pittsburgh that also triggered a move on defense. The next practice after the Steelers game, Jeremiah Trotter was back at middle linebacker and Simoneau was moved to the weak side. Coordinator Jim Johnson had wanted to make the move, but didn't want to disrupt a team that was on the way to 7–0. Once the Eagles lost, the move was made.

Trot was special. Coming from a small school (Stephen F. Austin) there was some relatability for me. With Trot it was hard for him to get on the field at first because how complicated Emmitt's defense was. It was complicated for everyone, but I remember the linebackers always saying how complicated it was for them. Trot was trying to learn and he was coming off a bad knee injury (from college). Then when Andy got here and Jim got here, he just took off. Trot became one of the best linebackers I ever played with. The way he played the game he was one of the most physical linebackers to ever play the game.

Then (in 2004) it was one of those things where you can't just start him off right away. It would have been a bad look. Mark Simoneau had been there all through training camp. But Trot knew the defense. And he was unique. He could do things that a lot of other linebackers couldn't do at that time. He was a problem for anyone who played against him. We used to call him the center killer. He was just that dominant when it came to what he did.

With Trotter back on defense and McNabb and Owens leading the offense the Eagles continued to roll. They won six straight after the loss in Pittsburgh and held three of those six opponents to seven points or less. That sixth win, a 12–7 decision over the Cowboys, came at an extremely high price. Owens was brought down with a horse-collar tackle and suffered a broken leg.

Yeah, (Dallas safety) Roy Williams and the Cowboy horse-collar shit. T.O. going down, it was worrisome for sure. But the good thing was, if there was anything good about him getting hurt, was the damage was done. We had clinched the top seed. And there was talk that he could come back. So we just had to hold serve until he came back.

With a 13–1 record, and the No. 1 seed in the NFC assured, Reid didn't need to see any of his other key players go down before the playoffs. So he rested most of the starters the final two weeks of the season and the team lost to the

St. Louis Rams and the Cincinnati Bengals. It was considered a controversial move to give the majority of the starters two weeks off plus the bye week. The concern was if they would be ready to turn it back on when the playoffs started. They were.

We played the Vikings first and that was a pretty good Vikings team, but we handled them. That was the game Freddie (Mitchell) balled out. The game where afterwards he thanked his hands. Freddie was out there. Like I said before, pure comedy.

Mitchell, getting more snaps in place of the injured Owens, caught five passes and scored a touchdown as the Eagles won easily, 27–14. Westbrook ran for 70 yards on 12 carries and caught five passes for another 47 yards. And McNabb went 21-for-33 for 286 yards and two touchdowns. Defensively, Trotter and Ike Reese each intercepted Daunte Culpepper passes. The win sent the Eagles to the NFC Championship Game for the fourth straight year. This time, the opponent would be the Atlanta Falcons, who crushed the Rams, 47–17, the week before. The three previous championship game losses to the Rams in St. Louis and to the Buccaneers and Panthers at home played on the team's mind.

I remember waking up that morning of the Atlanta game and I was nervous. Ner-vous. It was a case of been there, done that. And then what would happen if we didn't get past that game again this year. We had been there before and didn't win it. There was trepidation, for sure.

The Eagles scored first on a Dorsey Levens touchdown run in the opening quarter, but the Falcons answered. The Eagles led just 14–10 at the half, but used a dominating second-half defense to pull away for a 27–10 win. That defense held the Falcons to 202 total yards for the game, sacked Michael Vick four times, two by Burgess, and picked him off once (Dawkins). Offensively, tight end Chad Lewis caught two touchdown passes, the second of which resulted in a broken foot. The injury obviously kept him out of the Super Bowl. Westbrook ran for 96 yards and caught another five passes. The Eagles, after three near misses, were headed to the Super Bowl for the first time since 1980.

Chad was a hard worker. I remember when he was there early on with us. Then he got cut. Andy brought him back and that's when he flourished. He became a hell of a player. And then off the field, Chad was special, too. I remember when we went to Kory Stringer's funeral and Chad brought The Book of Mormon. It was the biggest book I had ever seen. What I appreciated about Chad was his story and his faith. He went on that mission at BYU. He just has a fascinating story. And Chad is a guy who is your friend till the end. You might not see him, or even talk to him, for a year, or two, then when you see him it's like you pick up right where you left off with him.

Lewis' injury was the one damper on what was a hot night in Philadelphia. The Eagles had broke through after the Three-Beat in the NFC Championship Games and were going to the Super Bowl. It had been a 24-year drought and it was finally over.

I just remember going through the city that night. We went to Capital Grill for dinner and the city was just abuzz. It was a great feeling all around. It was like, "Finally." For me, I reflected on all the great players who came before me who never went to a Super Bowl, never got the chance to go. And here I was going to the Super Bowl. And no matter what happens, I'm getting the chance to play in the Super Bowl.

Things happen for a reason. If Douglas would have had a better experience in Jacksonville he would have never gone back to Philadelphia. If he had signed with Kansas City he would have likely still been a Chief.

It was crazy, right. My biggest fear initially was (the Eagles) going to the Super Bowl without me. Now, I get the opportunity to go back there and now we are going to the Super Bowl. It just felt right. It felt like that's how it was supposed to be.

CHAPTER 15

SUPER BOWL XXXIX

T.O. was going to play. So that got us excited. He was practicing hard the week before because he really wanted to play. He looked good. Everyone was asking if T.O. was going to play. They tried to keep it under wraps, but we knew he was going to play.

Terrell Owens not only played in Super Bowl XXXIX, he starred. If the Eagles could have pulled off the upset of the New England Patriots there's no doubt he would have been the game's Most Valuable Player. Playing in his first game just six weeks after having surgery to repair a broken fibula and a torn ligament in his ankle, Owens caught nine passes for 122 yards in the Eagles 24–21 loss. He was on the field for 63 of the Eagles 72 offensive snaps.

We knew we were going against history with (quarterback Tom) Brady and (head coach Bill) Belichick. For me personally, I didn't know how it was going to play out. We knew how good the Patriots were. We had a chance to see them before the dynasty started when we played the Rams (in the 2001 NFC Championship Game) and lost that game and then the Patriots beat the Rams. So we knew we were going against greatness, but we knew we had a chance. We had T.O. back. The fact that T.O. came back and was able to do what the was able to do, that was phenomenal. I don't care what anyone says. That was phenomenal.

Super Bowl week began the way it always does, with a lot of media hype. From the Eagles side, most of it surrounded Owens as word got out he was going to try to play. There was some on Douglas, however, as this Super Bowl was going to be played in, of all places, Jacksonville.

We got to Jacksonville before everyone else, so we had a little time to get some things done. It doesn't ramp up until later in the week. And there was nothing really that we wanted to see, or needed to see. For Florida it was a little cold and it wasn't that much fun because it was Jacksonville. I remember some family members complaining about the hotel where they stayed. Somebody left some dirty drawers in one of the rooms. So that was a big thing. Simona (Hugh's wife) called me and she's freaking out. Saying she's not going to stay at this place. So her and some other families rented a house. The conditions, they said, were just awful.

You're not supposed to have to deal with family during Super Bowl week. But for us it was just bad. All the kids were young at that time and it was just bad. So we had to deal with all of that. The bottom line is it was a business trip and that's how we tried to treat it.

And for Douglas there was unfinished business in the city he couldn't wait to leave and was now headed back to for the biggest, and what turned out to be last, game of his career.

The irony is crazy. To go back to Jacksonville and to know the city the way I did, it was a little nuts. Jacksonville was going into the 1950s and not in a good way. It's in a time warp. They care more about college football than they do the NFL. I think that's obvious. It was just a different place. They brought those cruise ships in to house everyone. It was just a crazy week.

New England, which was looking to go back-to-back after beating Carolina in Super Bowl XXXVIII and also win its third Super Bowl in four years, was installed as an early six-point favorite over the Eagles. The line quickly moved to seven and stayed there until kickoff. The Patriots went 14–2 during the regular season but were only the AFC's No. 2 seed since Pittsburgh and rookie quarterback Ben Roethlisberger went 15–1, including that blowout of the Eagles in the middle of the season. Brady and the Pats had no problem with Payton Manning and the Colts in their playoff opener, winning 20–3 and then went into Pittsburgh and put a 41–27 whipping on the top seed Steelers in the AFC Championship Game.

The Eagles, however, did not lack confidence. They had Owens, who had an incredible first season with the team, back. And McNabb, now with a legitimate No. 1 wide receiver, had the best season of his career. Owens, despite missing the last two games of the regular season, caught 77 passes for 1,200 yards and 14 touchdowns. The 77 receptions were the fourth most by an Eagles wide receiver at the time. The 1,200 yards were the second most and the 14 touchdowns are still the most ever by an Eagles receiver. And he missed two games. McNabb, who played just one series in the Week 15 loss to the Rams and not at all in the Week 16 loss to the Bengals, completed a career best 64 percent of his passes for at the time a career-best 3,875 yards with a career-best 31 touchdowns. Both were named to the Pro Bowl along with running back Brian Westbrook on offense. The young, rebuilt defense, sent middle linebacker Jeremiah Trotter, cornerback Lito Sheppard and safeties Brian Dawkins and Michael Lewis to Hawaii.

We knew it wasn't going to be easy. They were really good. But we knew we had a chance.

Super Bowl XXXIX is the only Super Bowl to be tied after the first quarter (0–0), at halftime (7–7), and after three quarters (14–14). The Eagles struck first on a McNabb touchdown pass to tight end L.J. Smith, but Brady answered with a touchdown pass to David Givens. The Pats took the lead on a two-yard Brady TD to linebacker Mike Vrabel on a trick play. The Eagles got even when McNabb found Westbrook for a 10-yard touchdown pass. From there the Patriots took over. And the Eagles didn't answer until it was too late.

Corey Dillon scored on a two-yard touchdown run and Adam Vinatieri kicked a 22-yard field goal to make it 24–14 with 5:40 to play. The Eagles, down two scores and with less than six minutes to play, did not go to a hurry-up offense, or even to shotgun formation. McNabb lined up under center every play, huddled after every play, and even after, on the 13th play of the drive, he hit slot receiver Greg Lewis with a beautiful 30-yard touchdown pass to make it 24–21, left just 1:48 on the clock. There were conflicting reports as to what exactly happened. Center Hank Fraley told WIP radio a few days after the game that McNabb had gotten sick on the drive. The quarterback was hit on four of his first five passes, one a vicious hit from Pats linebacker Ted Bruschi. The quarterback would say later the hit by Bruschi took its toll on him. Reid admitted much later that the team could have shown more urgency and perhaps he should have gone no-huddle. But quickly added that they did eventually score. It just didn't happen quickly enough.

It was a back-and-forth affair. You heard stuff after the game. Donovan got sick. Donovan threw up. This happened. That happened. I didn't see any of it. That's me. Then there were rumors that he was out partying the night before and that's why he got sick. Again, I didn't see any of that. People like to embellish and especially with Donovan they like to embellish. I don't think the night before the most important game of his career he was out partying. I just can't see that from him. I can't. That's not Donovan. I know I wasn't out. I had my butt at the hotel all night.

The Eagles tried an unsuccessful onside kick after the 30-yard touchdown pass. New England ran the ball three times, forced the Eagles to take their two remaining time outs, and punted them back to the 4-yard line with just 46 seconds left. With 17 seconds left, McNabb took one last shot downfield for Smith, but it was a bit high, glanced off the tight end's fingers, and was intercepted by safety Rodney Harrison. And that was it.

For the game McNabb completed 30 of 51 passes for 357 yards with three touchdowns and three interceptions. New England took away Westbrook and the running game. The Pro Bowl back carried 15 times for 44 yards and 22 of those yards came on the final play of the first half as the Eagles ran out of the clock. Take that away and it was 14 carries for 22 yards. Brady was 23 of 33 for 236 yards with two touchdowns. Dillon ran for 75 yards on 18 carries and the game's MVP, wide receiver Deion Branch, caught 11 of Brady's passes for 133 yards.

It was tough for me personally because I knew it was probably my last game. I remember being out on the field and seeing the confetti falling and thinking it's the wrong color. I was trying to find solace, knowing this is probably my last go-round and I was like, "Hey, at least I got a chance to be in this game." It wasn't the outcome I wanted. But again, how many great players have never even gotten to this point. And I was in it. So I took some solace in that, not a whole lot, but hey, if this was how it was supposed to be, so be it.

The 2004 season was Douglas 10th, a lifetime by NFL standards. He would turn 34 in August before what would have been an 11th season. There was also the shoulder injury that still required surgery and the knee that would probably never be a full 100 percent again.

When you get to a certain age it all starts to matter. Like, I waited to get the surgery, because I wanted to play. If I would have gotten it right away I might have been able to steal a couple more seasons. But I wanted to play. I wanted to play that year. I wanted the chance to go to the Super Bowl.

CHAPTER 16

T.O.

It was 20 years ago. It's kind of crazy to think that with everything I've accomplished in my career and people still want to talk about what happened with me and T.O. from 20 years ago.

What's really hard to believe is that Terrell Owens played just 21 games—22 if you include Super Bowl XXXIX—for the Philadelphia Eagles. With everything that happened in that span it felt more like 21 years.

That's all it was? Twenty-two games. Wow.

When the Eagles acquired Owens in that round-about trade with San Francisco and Baltimore they signed him to a seven-year deal worth $49 million, $9 million of which he earned in 2004. Most observers, including those with the NFL Players Association, advised Owens not to take the very team-friendly deal. The ever self-confident Owens took it and figured he would outplay the contract in a year and renegotiate. So after his brilliant 2004 season and incredible performance on one leg in the Super Bowl he tried to do just that. The Eagles, at least Joe Banner's Eagles, didn't play that game. They did not renegotiate a seven-year deal after just one year. Owens and his newly hired agent, Drew Rosenhaus, pleaded his case. They brought up his stats, his presence on the team, and perhaps suggested that Banner re-watch the Super Bowl. The team president and chief negotiator smiled and suggested they come back in another five years or so. Worse than that, Banner would leak word to his media cronies that how dare a player come in after just one year and want to renegotiate a seven-year deal.

That was Joe. That was all Joe.

That lit the fuse under the ultra-sensitive Owens. Which led to everything from his ripping anyone and everyone around the team. Head coach Andy Reid sent him home from training camp one day and he proceeded to hold a press conference on the front lawn of his home in Moorestown, New Jersey, where he did sit-ups and Rosenhaus answered every question with, "Next question." No one was safe. The front office, offensive coordinator Brad Childress, (who he humiliated and embarrassed in meetings), quarterback Donovan McNabb ("I wasn't the one who got tired in the Super Bowl"), and anyone else who got in his way. That included a former player, now working for the team and doing local radio.

The Eagles gave me the title of Ambassador. I changed it to the Bad Assador. Yeah it was one of those things where I shook hands, kissed babies, all of that stuff.

On the field, Owens was still himself. He caught seven passes for 112 yards in the Monday night opener against the Atlanta Falcons in the Georgia Dome. He went for five catches for 143 yards and two touchdowns against his old team, the San Francisco 49ers. He had nine catches for 80 yards and a touchdown against the Oakland Raiders and followed that with 11 catches for 171 yards against the Kansas City Chiefs. And in what turned out to be his final game as an Eagle he caught three passes for 154 yards and a touchdown against the Denver Broncos. For the season, despite playing in just seven games, he led the Eagles in receiving yards (763) and touchdown catches (6).

It was a game against Dallas, a bad game, a 33–10 loss, where Owens' off the field actions finally caught up to him and turned the ultimate fan favorite into a villain. It was straight out of the WWE. Owens left the Cowboys AT&T Stadium that Sunday night, after a brutal loss, wearing a Michael Irvin throwback jersey. If you know even a little bit about the Eagles/Cowboys rivalry you know that's not going to fly in Philadelphia. And it didn't. Owens wanted out and tried everything. Finally it may have worked. If the Cowboys jersey didn't do the trick, everything that followed it did.

I've heard T.O. tell the story several times. I'm not saying T.O. is a liar. But he misremembers a lot that went on with that story.

What happened was this. It all started when the Eagles went to Dallas and lost. They got trounced and T.O. is wearing a Michael Irvin jersey. I'm on the radio that Monday with Angelo Cataldi, the *WIP Morning Show* host. You know Angelo. Well, he just went on a rant that Monday morning. And it's unfortunate for me that I'm sitting there while Angelo is going on this rant on T.O. I'm not defending him. But I'm not stopping Angelo, either. I had just started on the radio. I hadn't been doing it that long. And Angelo is the main guy at the station. He's the man. Now again, I did not defend T.O., because there was nothing to defend. T.O. did what he did. I'm trying to the best of my ability to say he's not really like that. I forget exactly what Angelo was saying, but it was like: he's not an Eagle, he's a bad guy, all of that kind of stuff. And I'm doing what I can to be a devil's advocate under the circumstances.

I go to the (NovaCare) complex later to hang out a while. Rick Burkholder (the Eagles trainer) had been listening to the radio. Everyone there listens to the radio. They might say they don't, but they do. He sees me. We talk and I tell him there wasn't much I could do to defend T.O. You can't defend that.

I'm in Rick's office and T.O. walks past and says something to the affect of, "We got a hater in the building." I didn't say anything initially. I knew he was talking to me. Then he came through again and said something else. But I didn't hear exactly what he said.

At this point I'm like, "Okay, he wants the smoke. He's making this bigger than what it is." Then, I figured it out. Someone must have called him and told him I said something about him. I was guilty by association. And that's the problem. Everyone wants to believe some random-ass person who tells them something, instead of just coming to me. He didn't come to me. He just believed what he heard. And I was already on the outs with T.O. He was mad at me because while he was in that contract dispute someone asked me what I would do. I answered and said I would come to work. If it was me, I would come to work. But I was a defensive end. Back then defensive ends didn't hold out. That's all I said. T.O. took that as I was against him. Because of that he thought I was against him from the start. That's how it was with T.O. you were either with him or against him. There was nothing in between.

So he's saying stuff. Now he goes in the hydro pool. This is at the time where T.O. was punking everyone. See he wants to play like he's the victim. But he was punking everyone. Ripping Donovan. Talking crazy to Andy at practice and everything. Now he comes to me and starts talking trash. I said, "I'm not the one." So I go into the hydro room to see him and said, "I don't know who the fuck you think you are, but I'll beat your fucking ass. I don't give a fuck. I don't play for the Eagles anymore. And I'm damn sure not scared of you." Or something to that affect. He gets out of the pool and at that point I realized I fucked up. I'm on their turf. I'm in their locker room and I'm disrupting things. I felt bad. Now people, some front-office guys, some players, see me and they see me being animated. I apologized to them. Because number one I should not have been in there.

Now T.O. comes back and says, "What do you want to do?" At this point we square up. We're about to come to blows. The only question now is who swings first. I'll be damn if I'm going to get caught with a punch. So I swing first and I miss. He swung. He missed. Now, we tussle. It's a pretty good tussle. And I'll never forget this. Trot (Jeremiah Trotter) grabbed me. And you know Trot is strong as hell. He has me in a headlock. I thought Trot was my friend and he's about to get me beat up. And then Trot yells, "Somebody grab T.O."

They grabbed T.O. And I said something like, "I was about to beat your ass."

After it was over I walked through the locker room. Donovan walked past me and said, "What happened?" I said me and T.O. got into a tussle.

Then T.O. came over and said, "If anyone else wants some, you can get some too."

I look at Donovan and I'm like, "He's not talking to me. We just had our moment. He's talking to you."

And it all started because somebody told him I said something about him. And I never did. Everyone started to hear about it, rumors spread, all of this and that. And I felt bad about it. I really did. Now there's this action where they are going to throw T.O. off the team. It was all just unfortunate. And it became "Us against T.O." And you had different camps, certain camps were for T.O. and certain camps were against T.O. It split the team. When I think back on it, it was ridiculous.

To this day people can say I whooped his ass or he whooped my ass. It doesn't matter. I always respected what he did and what he did for the team. I've told him that. And we've talked sparingly through the years. I've told him, "You handled it wrong." He tells the story the way he wants to tell it. But I always said if I was ever starting a team, T.O. would be one of the first guys I would want. He's a ride-or-die dude. He's as loyal as they come. He's different. But what wide receiver isn't?

(After the incident) It was just like a flood of emotions came out. It made me look at him differently. There was more to it than just that. And I felt bad about the whole thing.

Seven games into the season with a 4–3 record, the Eagles suspended Owens for four games without pay. Not long after his tussle with Douglas, Owens went on ESPN and called the Eagles "classless" for not recognizing his 100th career touchdown. And in the same interview again took a shot at McNabb when he said the team "Would be better off with Brett Favre at quarterback."

The following Monday, after a loss to Washington dropped the Eagles to 4–4, Reid told the media after the four-game suspension the star receiver would be inactive for the rest of the year. "We gave Terrell every opportunity to avoid this outcome," Reid said.

With Owens out of the picture, the Eagles floundered. It got worse when McNabb went down with a sports hernia injury and was replaced by backup quarterback Mike McMahon. The team won just two of its final eight games, finished the season 6–10, and went from NFC champions to last place in the NFC East. They missed the playoffs for the first time since 1999, Reid's first year. In the 22 games Owens played for the Eagles they went 17–5.

It's just unfortunate the situation went bad between him and Donovan. And I don't know why. It should be at this point that we should be able to move past it. But to this day they're still not close. We had an opportunity, and we did some beautiful things when they were together, no question about it. But it's unfortunate when you think about that era. It's unfortunate that people only think about the negative shit.

At first him and Donovan were cool. And again I don't know what happened. I'm not in the offensive meeting rooms. Some people said it was jealousy. And I don't get it, I don't understand why. Because Donovan was the guy. And so was T.O. They were both at the top of their game. There wasn't any reason to be jealous. But for whatever reason they just couldn't co-exist together. If they would have played together another year Donovan would be in the Hall of Fame or he would at least had a good case for it.

McNabb and Owens arrived in Philadelphia to different music. When the team acquired Owens before the 2004 season fans chanted his initials in a sing-song manner from his first day of training camp throughout that 2004 Super Bowl season. When McNabb was selected with the No. 2 pick of the 1999 NFL Draft he was greeted with a chorus of boos from 30 Eagles fans who attended the draft in New York and wanted the team to pick Texas running back Ricky Williams. To a man, almost all 30 apologized to the quarterback. But he never seemed to get over it.

There may have been some other circumstances that mattered as well. When Owens was fighting for a new contract, McNabb never said a word. Which is fine, except he did go to bat for running back Brian Westbrook when he was looking for a new deal.

In T.O.'s mind if you weren't in support of him, you were the enemy. But where Donovan messed up was he supported Westbrook and he got paid. Donovan was a good dude, but he was different too. Donovan didn't say anything when Trot left, when I left, when none of us left. Donovan was (the Eagles) guy. He was that dude. Until he wasn't. T.O. was the catalyst for us to get over the hump. T.O. was the missing ingredient, no question he was the missing ingredient. You saw the difference in the team that Super Bowl year and it was because of T.O.

But yeah T.O. was different. He grew up different. He doesn't see things the way other people see things. And I understand that.

The question will never be answered. But until the Eagles finally made it back to a Super Bowl in 2017 and won it, you had to wonder what might have been if McNabb and Owens could have put aside whatever their differences were. Because on the field they seemed to be in step. I mean, when a guy gains 154 yards just before he gets suspended for the year, the off the field stuff certainly wasn't affecting his play. But again it was also the contract, the one Owens probably should have never signed and the one the Eagles refused to change. Isn't it always about the money?

You see what happened (after the Eagles won their second Super Bowl in 2024) and they gave (running back) Saquon Barkley more money (after just one year) for what he did. I'm surprised that hasn't been made more of a big deal. The irony is there. One cat gets rewarded for what he did. The other cat got ridiculed.

Twenty years is a long time. And while Owens and Douglas might not necessarily hang out together. There is certainly no bad blood. The incident in the locker room back in 2005 is forgotten unless an outsider mentions it.

We're cool. We are. We've talked. I was happy for him when he made the Hall of Fame. And I like the fact he did it his way by not showing up in Canton. That's T.O. That's his way.

Douglas also recalled his first encounter with Owens. It was after the 2000 season when both players were in Hawaii for the Pro Bowl. Douglas representing the Eagles and Owens the 49ers.

I remember my first year at the Pro Bowl they gave me the camera to film things. T.O. followed me around with the camera and I put him on camera every time he wanted. It didn't bother me. But it was weird because it was my first year and he wanted the camera on him. I was like, "Okay, he wants to be on camera, that's cool." But that let me know then he was a little different.

CHAPTER 17
ON THE RADIO

I was in camp but I felt run down. I remember telling Tra Thomas, "I'm not going to make it." I didn't bounce back the same. My body didn't feel the same. It was a grind just to go to practice.

Tra was like, "C'mon, man, I don't want to hear that, just suck it up." Tra was one of my best friends. He's just trying to get me mentally right and suck it up. But I'm telling him, no this is different. My shoulder was still messed up, but it wasn't just my shoulder. It was my whole body. I didn't bounce back. I didn't recover. You know when you go to sleep and you wake up and you might be a little sore, but you're fine. I would wake up and I would still be fucked up. Something just wasn't right. I wasn't myself.

Douglas went to training camp with the Eagles in 2005, his second year back with the team. As he said, it wasn't the same. Ten years in the league had started to take its toll. It was time.

I didn't want to quit. I'm not a quitter.

And he didn't. The Eagles did it for him.

They got Trent Cole that year. And Trent was out there killing it. And I'm like, this young cat is going to take my job. I knew it was a rap in the preseason. It was the last game. We were playing the Jets. It was the third or fourth quarter and I'm out there. They're about to cut me. That's the sign. If you're playing late in the last preseason game, that's not good.

It was cool. I had a nice run; got to the Super Bowl. Now, it's time to figure out what I'm going to do next. My body was telling me it was time to go. And it was time to go for real.

Douglas got the call from Eagles personnel man Tom Heckert to go see Andy Reid and to bring his playbook. That's the end. Another call from another Eagles executive was a beginning.

(After I was released) I got a call from the Eagles. It was Joe Banner. I was sitting at home in Atlanta trying to figure out what to do and I actually got two calls. The Eagles called and WIP (radio) called. Howard

Eskin (the afternoon drive time host) called and said, "If you come back to Philly you have a job."

So my wife and I are sitting there and she was like, "Hugh, what are you going to do?"

I was like, "We could just stay here and chill.

She said, "You know you're not going to be happy doing that." I think she was saying that because she was really saying you're going to start to get on my nerves. Whatever it was she was like, "You need to do something."

The thing was we just built a house and we weren't there that long. But she was right. And I commend her for being able to up and move the way she did.

Douglas took both jobs. The Eagles gave him the job as a team Ambassador ("The Bad Assador") and WIP hired him as a fill-in co-host. He did the Morning Show *with Angelo Cataldi on Mondays during the football season and he worked some nights and weekends, usually paired with radio veteran Rob Charry.*

I didn't know what I wanted to do. I knew (radio) was easy. And it was fun. It wasn't like work, because I was just basically being myself. And between Howard and Angelo I learned a lot about radio, a tremendous amount. Those two really helped me.

WIP was old-school radio. It wasn't just about stats. Of course stats are part of it. But you have to be entertaining. People want to know you. What's funny is I'm out and people speak to me like they know me and I don't know them. They just feel like they talk to me every day.

It's not uncommon for former players to become radio hosts, especially in Philadelphia where several former Eagles, and Phillies, have graced the airwaves over the years. Douglas was one of the first (since linebacker Garry Cobb from the '80s). The tough part, of course, is putting aside your team loyalty and having to be critical of your old team, and teammates, at times.

If you're being fair in the job I'm doing, I can be critical and not make it sound personal. A lot of times in the job we do you hear guys say,

"He's garbage … he stinks … he's terrible." As long as I don't use those words and keep it in the realm of the game I'm all right. I remember when I was in Jacksonville Jeff Lageman (the Jaguars former defensive end and one of their better players who became a radio host) used to do that. He used to be critical, but it was cool for him to do that. He played the game. He would be critical but not personal. I think that's the most important thing. You have to remember these cats are human. They're just somewhat super human in their ability to do what they do. To me, I just want to be fair and balanced.

Sometimes that doesn't work. Some players expect more praise than criticism from a former teammate.

The first time I said something controversial I said it about Darwin (Walker, the Eagles veteran defensive tackle)). And Darwin didn't like it. He snatched me up when I came out to practice one day. We talked about it. It's different with defensive players, because they get it. And Darwin got it and that was the last time anything was said about it. Anyone who does this for a living is going to have to be critical to a certain extent. There are some people who are just super sensitive to any kind of criticism. And those people need to sit their butts down.

Talking football came easy for Douglas obviously. And while football dominates sports talk in Philly. There are times when you have to talk about the Phillies, the 76ers, and the Flyers as well. Especially the Phillies, since they went to back-to-back World Series in 2008 and 2009, during Douglas' initial run at WIP.

For me, I had to follow more baseball. But there's one thing that's constant throughout all of professional sports, and that's the level it takes to get to play those sports. That's universal. What's more intriguing, and Angelo taught me this, is we all talk about stat lines. We're all using the same stats. That's the facts. But what story angle do you want to tell when you talk about the game. Because at the end of the day it's entertainment. At first there were those dudes who were like you don't know this, you don't know that, you don't know the third. But if you played professional sports it's all kind of universal to get to that point. The story lines like what could be going through a player's head. Well, you've been there. You've gone through what he's going through, good and bad. I never played baseball, but I can give you an idea of what Bryce Harper is going through, positive or negative. It's all about perspective, it's not just black and white. There's a lot of gray.

While Douglas was learning the radio business, the Eagles were going through some ups and down from the 2006 to 2010 seasons. They made the playoffs in four of those five seasons. Two of the four playoff seasons ended in the first round, however, and the most unlikely one went the furthest. Donovan McNabb's Eagles career ended as well during that time span. Here's a look at each of those years.

2006
Jeff Garcia Saves the Day

McNabb, who missed time with a sports hernia injury in the disaster that was 2005, tore his ACL in a loss to Dallas that left the team 5–5. This year the team was better prepared for life without McNabb.

Veteran Jeff Garcia, who had been with the San Francisco 49ers and also drew the wrath of Terrell Owens, was signed before the season as the No. 2 quarterback. Garcia replaced McNabb in Week 11 and promptly lost to Peyton Manning and the Colts in a 45–21 rout. The team was now 5–6 and faced a three-game NFC East road trip at Washington, at New York and finally at Dallas on Christmas night.

First there was a Monday night game at home against the Carolina Panthers. The Eagles trailed 14–7 at the half and 21–14 after three quarters. The new quarterback then took over. Garcia, who threw for 312 yards and three touchdowns in the game, found Reggie Brown for a 40-yard touchdown to tie the game, 24–24, He then led the game-winning field goal drive, after Brian Dawkins picked off a Jeff Delhomme pass and returned it to the Panthers 37, for the 27–24 win. The Eagles were back even at 6–6. Then came the three-game road trip and the Eagles beat in order: Washington, 21–19; New York, 36–22 and Dallas, 23–7.

Against Washington Garcia threw two touchdown passes, one to tight end L.J. Smith and the other to wide receiver Donte Stallworth. Safety Michael Lewis had the play of the game with an 84-yard interception return for a touchdown.

Garcia completed 19 of 28 passes with a touchdown to Reggie Brown in the win over the Giants. Brian Westbrook led the offense with 97 yards rushing and two touchdowns and defensive end Trent Cole made it two pick-sixes in two weeks with a 19-yard interception return for a touchdown to put the game away.

Dallas' offense, which included wide receiver Terrell Owens, managed just 201 total yards in the Eagles rout. Westbrook again led the way with 122 yards rushing. Dawkins and Lito Sheppard both intercepted Tony Romo in the game.

That was the Merry Christmas Philadelphia year. I remember that. Philadelphia loved Jeff Garcia. Joe Conklin (Philadelphia comedian and a regular of the *WIP Morning Show*) made a song about him. It was a really funny song. What Garcia did was he got the ball out of his hands quickly and that was key. And he was just a spark for the team. You know it was a time when Donovan was getting hurt and people weren't feeling him like they once did. The team was starting to change. Garcia came in and was a breath of fresh air. He endeared himself to the city. People loved the way he played. He was gutsy, he had all of that.

(Brian) Westbrook (who ran for 1,217 yards and caught 77 passes for 699 yards) was balling, too. Andy gave him a chance to showcase what he can do. And it really paid off for him.

Garcia finished the regular season with a 24–17 win over Atlanta for a five-game winning streak and the NFC East division crown. His stat line read 65 percent completion rate with nine touchdowns and just two interceptions in his six starts.

In the first round against the Giants, it was Westbrook's 141 rushing yards that led to the 23–20 win. Garcia, with Westbrook running for 33 yards, completed two key passes on the game-winning drive that ended with a David Akers field goal with 0:00 on the clock.

The following week the Eagles lost at New Orleans, 27–24, as Garcia and the Eagles were outdueled by Drew Brees and the Saints. Garcia, who was on a one-year deal, left as a free agent to sign with Tampa Bay the ensuing offseason.

All in all that was kind of a good year, an interesting year.

2007

Eight was not Enough

Except for the running of Westbrook, who was establishing himself as one of the best backs in the league and one of the best Eagles of all-time, it was a dismal season for the Eagles.

Westbrook ran for 1,333 yards and caught 90 passes for 771 yards in a remarkable season.

McNabb (an 89.9 quarterback rating with 19 touchdowns and seven interceptions) missed two games with injury and the Eagles finished the season 8–8. It took three wins in the final three weeks of the season to get to .500. A 1–3 start led to 5–8 with three games to go and the team was never in serious playoff contention.

Donovan started to get banged up year after year. It was starting to take its toll on him and the team.

2008

A Wild Finish

This year started to resemble the previous year when the team had an ugly 13–13 tie against Cincinnati and then got blown out by Baltimore, 36–13, the following week to sit at 5–5–1.

After the Cincinnati game, McNabb admitted he didn't know a game could end in a tie and was getting ready for the second overtime. At halftime of the Baltimore game he got benched. Yeah, it was looking like that kind of year.

Until it didn't.

On Thanksgiving night, McNabb returned as the starter and the Eagles blew out Arizona, 48–20, and then beat the Giants and Browns to get to 8–5–1. All of a sudden they were alive in the wild-card chase. A loss to Washington made that dream a little tougher. Actually it was a lot tougher.

The Eagles went into the final week of the season needing all kinds of help to get to the postseason. Not only did they have to beat the Cowboys, who they had lost to earlier in the season, they needed help from unlikely sources. They needed the Chicago Bears to lose at Houston. Okay, that wasn't impossible. Houston was 7–8 and at home. And they also needed the Tampa Bay Bucs to lose at home to the 4–11 Oakland Raiders. That didn't seem like a good bet.

They got both by the same 31–24 score. Then they blew out Dallas, 44–6.

That was a wild day for sure.

It didn't stop there. In the playoffs, at 9–6–1, the Eagles went on the road and beat the Minnesota Vikings and head coach Brad Childress, their former offensive coordinator and Reid's close friend, 26–14. A 71-yard touchdown pass from McNabb to Westbrook midway through the fourth quarter put the game away.

The following week they upset the top-seed Giants, 23–11, outscoring the NFC East champs 10–0 in the fourth quarter to pull away. It wasn't much of an offensive affair. Cornerback Asante Samuel, who had a pick–6 the week before in Minnesota, had another interception of Eli Manning.

That sent the Eagles back to the NFC Championship Game for the fifth time in eight years. This one was in Arizona against a Cardinals team they had destroyed on Thanksgiving.

This time it was the Cards who celebrated with a 32–25 win. It was also the last game for defensive coordinator Jim Johnson, who died of cancer seven months later.

First thing I knew about Jim was I remembered him when he was in Seattle, him and (defensive line coach) Tommy (Brasher). They came to town my first year and beat the brakes off us. I remember saying, "I wish

I played in that defense." They had some players, too. And that's what we knew when Andy hired him, we were getting that guy from Seattle.

What made Jim easy to play for was he adapted to what we did. He let me play my game. He was never the type who was locked into one thing. The defense flowed the way the players he had flowed. He adapted to what we did. That's why Trot had the success he had. He let Trot be who Trot was. When you played a while you got used to doing things a certain way. You didn't want to change.

I loved him. We all loved him, especially the older guys they really loved him. I remember him and Troy Vincent used to have great talks about the defense and what they wanted to do.

It was sad when we got word (of his cancer). It happened fast. It happened real fast. It made you realize how precious time is. It really, really did.

2009
McNabb's Last Stand

This was a nightmare season for the Eagles and Eagles fans. They lost to the rival Cowboys three times that year and twice over the final seven days of the season.

On the last Sunday of the regular season the Eagles were in Dallas with the NFC East title in the balance. Unlike 2008, when everything went the Eagles way, nothing went right a year later. The Cowboys won, 24–0, and took the division at 11–5. The Eagles, at the same 11–5, would be a wild-card team because of Dallas' head-to-head sweep. Not only that, the Eagles had to head back to Dallas for a Saturday night first-round playoff game. The Cowboys won again, 34–14.

That was the air guitar game.

During introductions, television cameras showed McNabb playing an air guitar on his way through the tunnel onto the field. It also turned out to be the quarterback's last game as an Eagle. And it wasn't a good way to end.

The Eagles offense had four turnovers, including an interception and fumble by the quarterback, and was a combined 2-for-13 on third and fourth down. After a scoreless first quarter, Dallas led 27–7 at the half and the game, the season and McNabb's career as an Eagle was over.

On Easter Sunday night, the Eagles franchise quarterback was traded to the Washington Redskins for a 2010 second-round draft pick and a 2011 fourth-round draft pick.

The thing about Don being traded is number one, you never get traded within the division. That's like a cardinal sin. And he got traded within the division and got traded to the Redskins. How disrespectful was that? Usually when a player like that gets traded they go from the AFC to NFC or the other way around. Normally. Not only did he get traded in the conference, he got traded in the division. That was crazy.

When I heard about it I was like, "Wow." It was telling. It was really telling. Then they played that first year and Don won that first game (against the Eagles). But that was kind of it for him. In the long run, Andy won that one.

McNabb played just one season in Washington where the team won just five of his 13 starts. He finished with another year in Minnesota where in six starts the Vikings went 1–5.

2010
The Michael Vick Experience

Before the 2009 season the Eagles made one of the more controversial signings in franchise history when they came to terms on a deal with quarterback Michael Vick. The same Michael Vick they had beaten in the playoffs in 2002 and in the NFC Championship Game in 2004. Except this was a little different. Vick had just served prison time for his involvement and ownership of Bad Dogs Kennels, a dog fighting operation in Virginia.

Not only was the signing controversial, but was interesting from the fact the Eagles still had Donovan McNabb under contract in 2009 and also had

Kevin Kolb, who they drafted in the second round of 2007 to be McNabb's eventual replacement. Where did Vick fit?

He didn't play much at all in 2009. But after McNabb was traded he originally became Kolb's backup. That didn't last long. Kolb got knocked out in the Eagles season-opening loss to the Green Bay Packers when a hit by linebacker Clay Matthews left him with a concussion. Vick took over and looked like the old Vick.

In 12 games, he missed a few with injury himself, he competed 63 percent of his passes for 3,018 yards with 21 touchdowns and six interceptions. More importantly, he led the Eagles to a 10–6 record and the NFC East title.

It did surprise me a little (when the Eagles signed Vick). But I was happy for him, because I know Vick's story. It's also a testament to the kind of person Andy is. Andy did a great job keeping it to just football. Everybody knew about the dog fighting thing and how he was in prison. He came right out of prison and got another chance. And some people didn't want him to have that second chance. It was an interesting time for sure, until he started winning football games. And you saw him do everything in his power to change his narrative.

I really didn't know him until he came to the Eagles. I mean, you knew who he was, but I didn't know him personally. But he told me stories about what it was like being locked up and how terrifying it was for him. He wasn't in one of those fake jails, either. He was in jail for real, for real. Mike had been through a lot. He's grown a lot. And you could see it. He was a different person.

The Eagles again started slowly in 2010. They were 4–3 at their bye week and then won six of seven after the bye to get to 10–4. That 10th win was incredible. They beat the Giants, 38–31, in a game they trailed 31–10 with 8:17 left in the fourth quarter.

Vick threw a 65-yard touchdown pass to tight end Brent Celek, scored on a four-yard run, and threw a 13-yard touchdown pass to wide receiver Jeremy Maclin to make it 31–31.

Then came DeSean Jackson's miraculous 65-yard punt return as time expired that gave the Eagles the win and a season sweep of the Giants. When both teams finished the season 10–6, the Eagles won the division on the first tiebreaker.

Vick's heroics ended in the first round of the playoffs, however, when the NFC's sixth seed and eventual Super Bowl champion Green Bay and Aaron Rodgers topped Vick and the Eagles, 21–16.

CHAPTER 18

THE DREAM TEAM AND THE END OF AN ERA

Why didn't the Dream Team work? That's tough.

I'm thinking it had to be somewhat of a power struggle. It sounds like there had to be some kind of a power struggle to me. People pulling (the team) in two different directions. That's what it felt like. I mean I don't know that for sure. I wasn't there in Philly, I was in Bristol (at ESPN). But the more I think about it, it just seems like it was one person pulling the team in one direction and someone else pulling it in another. And that's not Coach Reid's style.

After the first-round playoff loss to the Green Bay Packers to end the 2010 season, the Eagles went on a free agent spending spree the following offseason. One of the players they added was quarterback Vince Young, the former University of Texas star and former first-round pick, to be Michael Vick's backup.

Young looked around his new locker room and saw Vick, running back LeSean McCoy, wide receivers DeSean Jackson and Jeremy Maclin and the new additions—running back Ronnie Brown, defensive tackle Cullen Jenkins, pass rusher Jason Babin, guard Evan Mathis, and the most sought after free agent in the league in 2011, cornerback Nnamdi Asomugha.

Asked during training camp what he thought about his new surroundings, Young called the 2011 Eagles, a "Dream Team."

You know what's funny? I was talking to Brandon Graham recently and he mentioned that Dream Team and how crazy it was.

What was also crazy was, again after the end of the 2010 season, a peculiar coaching move. Defensive coordinator Sean McDermott, who had replaced his mentor, the late Jim Johnson, was fired. Who was hired to take McDermott's place? Reid named his offensive line coach Juan Castillo as defensive coordinator. The headline on the back page of the Philadelphia Daily News *the next day read: WTF!*

I liked Juan as the offensive line coach. Juan was a good offensive line coach and everyone knew him as an offensive line coach. But to make him defensive coordinator? That was a stretch, man. I really don't know what was going on with Big Red when he did that. That one had a lot of people scratching their head. I don't know. Juan probably went in and lobbied for it, because that sounds like something he might do. And Andy probably just gave him the chance, because that's what Andy would do.

Or maybe not. Reid was asked the day after the playoff loss to the Packers if he anticipated any changes to his coaching staff. His answer was, unless someone was getting a head coaching spot, he expected the staff to be back intact. A few weeks later, while Reid was on vacation, the Eagles announced McDermott's firing. Was this Reid's decision? Or had the power struggle already begun? There was some speculation that team president Joe Banner didn't want McDermott and made the move to fire him. Reid, in somewhat retaliation, then named Castillo to replace him.

I get it now. Big Red was pretty straight up. If he said something he usually meant it. He didn't go out and do the opposite. So that does kind of make sense (that Banner was behind the firing).

McDermott would go on to join another former Eagles assistant and Johnson protégé, Ron Rivera, who was head coach of the Carolina Panthers. He would then parlay that Panthers defensive coordinator job into becoming head coach of the Buffalo Bills. Castillo? He was demoted midway through his second season and would go back to being an offensive line coach for several different teams.

What I remember about Sean is that he went to William and Mary and was there the same time as coach (Mike) Tomlin (of the Pittsburgh Steelers). And they were really close. Sean was a disciple of Coach Johnson, and that's why he got the job. But nobody was Coach Johnson. They tried to be, but Jim Johnson was different. That's just the reality of it. Jim was a special man.

So what exactly happened with the 2011 Eagles that Young dubbed the "Dream Team"? It wasn't anything good. In their opener they beat a Rams team that would finish 2–14. Then they quickly fell to 1–4 with losses to the

Falcons, the Giants, the 49ers, and the Bills. They hit a low at 4–8 before winning their last four games to salvage an 8–8 season.

Vick, who regained his magic in 2010, was just okay in 2011, with an 84.9 quarterback rating that included 18 touchdown passes and 14 interceptions. Young, forced to start three games, had a rating of 60.9 and threw more than twice as many interceptions (9) as touchdown passes (4). It was also his final year in the league. The other additions didn't amount to much, either. And the worst was the one who was supposed to be the best. Asomugha, a four-time All-Pro and a shutdown cornerback with the Raiders, just never fit in with the Eagles defense or in the locker room. Reports came out after the season that he would regularly eat his lunch alone in his car.

Nnamdi wasn't the guy they thought they were getting.

Owner Jeffrey Lurie held a press conference at the end of the season and issued a warning, perhaps to his head coach, that "8–8 is not good enough."

When the team followed that 8–8 2011 season by going 4–12 in 2012 it was the end of Reid's 14-year run with the Eagles. The winningest coach in team history was fired the day after a season-ending loss to the New York Giants.

Rich Kotite's final season as head coach of the Eagles, 1994, was the greatest collapse in NFL history. The team went from 7–2 to 7–9. And is still the only team to ever start a season 7–2 and finish it under .500.

Ray Rhodes' final season as head coach of the Eagles, 1998, was the losingest season in team history as the Eagles finished 3–13.

Reid's last season, 2012, may have been worse than Kotite's and Rhodes." Two one-point wins to open the season—over Cleveland (17–16) and Baltimore (24–23)—and a two-point win (19–17) over the New York Giants in Week 4 got the Eagles to 3–1. They would then win just one of their last 12 games—a 23–21 decision over Tampa Bay. Add it up. Their four wins were by a combined six points. They were a touchdown away from being 0–16. The offense and defense both ranked 29th in the league in scoring.

Vick won just three of his 10 starts, threw 12 touchdown passes with 10 interceptions, and had a quarterback rating of 78.1. Rookie quarterback

Nick Foles started six games and won one with six touchdowns and five interceptions and had a quarterback rating of 79.1. McCoy led the running game with 840 yards and Maclin was the leading receiver with 857 yards.

I was at ESPN during those years and I used to talk to (former Eagles quarterback from the late '70s and early '80s) Ron Jaworski all the time because he was up there at the same time I was. And we would eventually talk about the Eagles. I remember when they were talking about firing Andy. That first year the Eagles weren't really doing great and the next year was worse. That Dream Team didn't work out the way they hoped. Juan was defensive coordinator. It was like, "Is Coach Reid losing it?"

Something certainly wasn't right. But it still was a shock to some when the Eagles fired Reid. At the press conference when Lurie made the announcement he followed it by saying he couldn't wait to put the coach in the team's Hall of Fame. Those two things—firing and Hall of Fame—don't usually go in the same sentence.

When Andy got fired I was a little upset. But what I remember was people were talking about it before it happened and I was like, "Andy's not getting fired."

And Jaworski says, "Hey, Hugh, it might be time for the coach to move on, his message has gotten stale." I remember that like it was yesterday.

I liked Coach Reid. I had my most success with him. So I was feeling some kind of way about him being fired. I was a little salty about it. I was upset. But Jaws might have been right. And he also said, "Don't worry about Andy, he'll land on his feet." And it worked out good for him.

Reid was fired by the Eagles, December 30, 2012. He was hired by the Kansas City Chiefs less than a week later, January 4, 2013. There was an interview with the Arizona Cardinals somewhere in between the two as well.

He was getting another job, it was just a matter of where. He went to Kansas City and, wow, look at what's happened.

As of the 2025 season, Reid took the Chiefs to nine straight AFC West titles (2016–2024), seven AFC Championship Games, five Super Bowl appearances, and three Super Bowl wins. He had the same kind of regular-season success in Philadelphia—six NFC East titles and nine playoff appearances—but couldn't get it done in the postseason.

Right now people in Philadelphia are mad at Coach Reid because he didn't win a Super Bowl here and then went and won in Kansas City. But you know how people say, "Your starter wife." It was like a starter wife. The thing is, you learn from the mistakes you made. You make mistakes and learn from them and get better from it. That's what Coach Reid did. He learned from the mistakes he made in Philly. I mean, he was a good coach in Philly, but he made some mistakes.

One of coach's blind spots, especially early on, was at the wide receiver position. You knew it, but you didn't say anything about it. It was Coach Reid and you didn't want to question it. But that was a blind spot for him. He corrected it in Kansas City. He went out and got Tyreek Hill and spent high picks on receivers. And he got the tight end, Travis Kelce. And then, of course, he got the quarterback, (Patrick) Mahomes.

Coach Reid could always coach. Was he stubborn? Yes. But he learned and he adapted. After he lost to the Buccaneers in the Super Bowl, he went out and got some offensive linemen.

He learned to flow like water and change things up as much as you can. I applaud him for that. I just wish, I just wish his ass would have been like that when we had the opportunity to win one here. Because if he did we could have won something.

In Philadelphia, Reid was the master of coming close. Three straight losses in the NFC Championship Game and then another loss in Super Bowl XXXIX. In Kansas City he's become a Hall of Fame coach with all that he's accomplished. And some of that is because he changed. He adapted.

After our losses to the Rams and Tampa Bay (in the NFC Championship Games), yeah, he should have started changing some stuff. And what I heard about when they finally signed T.O. was that wasn't (Reid's) decision. He didn't go after T.O. That came from over his head. He thought they were okay (at wide receiver) with what they had. And someone said bullshit, no we're not. So he got T.O. and went to a Super Bowl. And now in Kansas City you see what he's done and it all worked.

CHAPTER 19

THE WORLDWIDE LEADER

It was a good opportunity. They liked me. They liked that I had an opinion. They liked that I wasn't afraid of Skip Bayless. And that I was not afraid to share my opinions.

As the Andy Reid era was coming to an end for the Eagles and the team was about to go through a major transition, Hugh Douglas' career was taking off in another direction. After doing work on Philadelphia radio and TV and some games for the NFL Network, ESPN called. How could he say no?

It started with Brian Jacobs, who was my agent, and his group. (ESPN) called him and wanted me to go up there and do a segment. So I did a segment of *First Take* (with Skip Bayless). That's when Skip was at his height, was in his heyday. I was not afraid to share my opinions and they liked that.

It was cool. I was doing a little this and that. Then they started a show called *Numbers Never Lie*. They wanted me to do the show. But in order for me to do it, I had to move to Bristol. So I moved to Bristol.

When the show began in 2011, Douglas was one of three hosts, along with former Boston-area sportswriter Michael Smith and former college basketball star and ESPN host Jalen Rose.

It was fun. But working at ESPN, they like controversy. Even on *First Take*, Skip would have his take and then they would massage the other takes. Because it's no fun if everyone agrees. It became more of trying to figure out how to have different takes and have a little bit of controversy.

To me, everything we do, even today, is semantics. It's the wording. You change a couple of words, it changes the meaning. It does for me anyway. So we would be in meetings and it would be, "How do you feel about this?" And I would say I feel this way. So basically they wanted you to take the other side. And it was fine for a while. As far as I knew it was fine. I enjoyed it immensely. I always come from the perspective, my opinion is mine. You don't have to agree with it. You don't have to like it. You don't have to like how I came to my conclusion. But it's mine. And I own that shit. My opinion is mine.

Numbers Never Lie *did well, at least Douglas thought it was doing well. Then there came a change when Rose left the show. What happened after that led to trouble.*

Jalen gets the opportunity to go to Los Angeles to do a show. So he leaves and the show dynamic changes. Jemele Hill (a sportswriter from the Detroit area) comes on board. I worked with her before and never had a problem with her. I didn't have a problem with her or Mike. Obviously, they had a problem with me that I didn't know about. The thing is they never said anything to me directly. People who watched the show would tell me, "Mike doesn't like you." "There's something weird going on with you and Mike."

I would say, "No, if he didn't like me he would tell me." Because we sat and talked every day. I was in a space where I admired both of them for what they did. They were journalists. I never knew they had a problem with me. I really didn't know.

Until it was too late.

A couple of times it would get a little contentious on the show, but I never took it any kind of way. I'm like, shit, this is a big-ass dinner table at ESPN, everyone is eating. I'm not mad about anything. This goes on like this for a while. It was always brought to me that they're not trying to replace me, it's all good. So to me everything was cool.

But it wasn't. Back door politics were beginning to take shape and Douglas, the former player and "non-journalist," was the target.

What ended up happening was Galen (Gordon) was the producer. I had had a run-in with Galen before. So this is where the story starts. They (Smith and Hill) were trying to get Galen. They didn't like Galen. I didn't like Galen either, but I wasn't about to shit on Galen just because they didn't like him. Galen used to be on *First Take* and him and Skip fell out over something. Skip got him off *First Take* and he moved to our show. Then him and Mike started bumping heads in meetings. It got to the point where they were trying to get Galen fired. Now, I didn't like him, either, like I said, but I wasn't going to try to get him fired. Mike and Jemele had this grand scheme to get him fired and I never got on board with it. Then I get called in the office and they tried to get me to say something bad about Galen. I just said, Galen needs to leave us alone and let me do my thing. In my book, I'm not going to get someone fired just because I don't like him. That's not cool.

Now a few days later Galen calls me in his office and he says to me, Jemele and Mike don't like you. I thought he was lying, because I felt if they didn't like me they would say something to me. He said they didn't like the way I worked and didn't like the way I prepared. I was like, whatever. So immediately after that meeting I went to Jemele and Mike and told them I just left Galen's office, and if there's a problem you have with me let me know. I could adjust and I will adjust accordingly. It didn't dawn on me until years later that Jemele wasn't upset because I came to her and talked about adjusting. She was upset because (Galen) told me what they'd talked about. I was looking at it like, if I need to change to help the show, I'm willing to do that. But that wasn't the case. They didn't want me to change. They wanted me out. They wanted my ass out of there.

It all came to a head at the 2013 National Association of Black Journalists Convention in Orlando.

We go to the NABJ. I'm there. They're there. Mike and Jemele were on stage. I tried to get on stage. The young lady (running the show) wouldn't let me on stage. Okay, not a problem. When Mike got off the stage, I said, "Mike, what's up?"

Mike put his finger in my face and said, "Don't you ever do that again." And he walks away.

I was like, "Mike, you all right?" I told him, I turned him around and told him, if you ever put your finger in my face again, I don't give a fuck about none of this, I will beat your motherfucking ass in front of all these people. I said it just like that.

He starts yelling, "I'm going to get you fired. I'm getting you fired. You watch, I'm getting you fired."

Galen was there and he says, "What's up with Mike?"

I said, "I don't know, he's mad about something."

Now remember, they were just trying to get Galen fired about a week ago. Now the tables are turned. Galen is aligned with them to fire me. I leave the venue (where the convention was being held) and go back to the hotel. Next morning I call him and he doesn't answer his phone. You know when you go somewhere and you know everyone is talking about you? I go down to breakfast and everyone is whispering. I had an early flight anyway, so I figured I better leave now. Because if I see this cat (Smith) and he acts the fool, I'm going to beat his ass. And I don't need that.

Now I'm back in Connecticut and my agent calls me. He said, "What did you do to Mike?" I said we got into an argument and my agent said, "He's trying to get you fired. He said you were drunk and belligerent at this function.

I said, "I wasn't drunk. Everyone had a few drinks, but I wasn't drunk."

After the call from my agent, (ESPN host and star) Stephen A. Smith called me and—I'll never forget this—he said, "They are trying to get you fired." He said, "I don't know what happened or what you did, but they're trying to get you fired. You need to call anyone who was there who can vouch for you."

I was like, "Oh shit." I called a few people, maybe three, and they all said the same thing, I wasn't what (Smith and Hill) said I was. (The ESPN people) waited a few days and the narrative changed. It became, I called (Smith) an Uncle Tom. I never did that. I never called him anything. I told them I did threaten to beat his ass. But I never called him Uncle Tom. I've never used that term. That's not how I talk. I did say, "I'll beat your ass." But I never hit him.

The ESPN brass took Smith's and Hill's side of the story and Douglas was out of a job that he not only enjoyed, but was very good at doing.

They got me out of there. The president called me into his office, and I'll never forget it because I got dressed up to get fired. I put on a suit to get fired. I talked to the HR person, but they had already made up their mind. They basically said: You're a big person, you're intimidating, and you did this, that and the third. And I kept saying I didn't do any of that. They didn't want to hear it. Mike was adamant about them firing me. That was the point he was trying to make, that he had pull. He wanted to show me he had pull.

It's been over 12 years since the incident occurred and Douglas lost his job until the writing of this book in 2025. He's never gotten it cleared as to what exactly happened or why it happened. Although, he has his ideas.

I have never spoken to Mike or Jemele since. She corroborated his story and she wasn't even there when it happened. I heard she wrote something about me in her book that nobody read, but no, I have not seen or talked to either one of them.

I've been in this business twenty-something years now so I must be doing something right. My thought is they just didn't like the way I did what I did. I'm assuming that because they came from a writer's background and they were more learned than me and I came off the cuff sometimes and spoke my mind. They didn't like that. In their eyes I didn't prepare the way they did. I was beneath them.

While Douglas was still at ESPN, the Eagles went from Andy Reid to another high-profile head coach in Chip Kelly, who had taken the college football world over with an offense that hadn't been seen before, or at least in a long time. Kelly, who turned the University of Oregon from an also-ran in the Pac 12 to a national power, had been in high demand by NFL teams but turned down interview requests and job offers every season. Until 2013, when he sat down with Jeffrey Lurie and Howie Roseman for a long interview. Roseman, who began his role in the Eagles front office as a salary-cap person, had moved up and was the team's general manager. He also replaced Joe Banner as Lurie's most trusted front office man.

Kelly originally turned down the Eagles offer and the team was reportedly ready to look elsewhere—the rumor was Gus Bradley, the Seattle Seahawks defensive coordinator—when a sudden change of direction had the Oregon coach on the next flight to Philadelphia.

I remember I didn't like the hire. I sent Howie a text and told him that. Kelly was a good college coach, but that was college. This was the NFL. It was different. Howie texted me back and said this guy was a good coach period.

Kelly's first year went as the Eagles hoped. He took the team that went 4–12 in Reid's final season to the NFC East title and a home playoff game. Quarterback Michael Vick was injured throughout the year, which opened the door for Nick Foles, who won eight of his 10 starts and threw 27 touchdown passes with just two interceptions. LeSean McCoy ran for 1,607 yards and DeSean Jackson had 1,332 yards receiving. The team, after an exhilarating opening win over Washington on Monday Night Football, *fell to 1–3. They got to 6–5 at their bye week and then won four of their last five to win the division.*

With the division title came a home playoff game against the New Orleans Saints. A Foles three-yard touchdown pass to tight end Zach Ertz gave the Eagles a 24–23 lead with under five minutes to play in that first-round playoff game But poor special teams allowed Darren Sproles, who would sign with the Eagles the following season, to bring the ensuing kickoff back 39 yards, and a horse-collar tackle by Cary Williams added 15 more. The Saints held the ball for nine plays, ran down the clock, and Shayne Graham kicked a 32-yard field goal with 0:03 to play for a 26–24 New Orleans win.

Things never got better for the Chip Kelly Eagles. They won 10 games again in 2014, but missed the playoffs. The following year they were 6–9 with a week to go when Lurie fired Kelly, citing his inability to get along with people in the building. The main person was Roseman.

In the general manager's mind, he and Kelly would be a new version of the Giants George Young and Bill Parcells, or the Packers Ron Wolf and Mike Holmgren. Or any other top-of-the-line GM and HC. Kelly had other ideas. He brought his own personnel man, Tom Gamble, with him to Philadelphia. Kelly thought in time he and Gamble would take over and oust Roseman. But Roseman fired Gamble at the end of the 2014 season. For a year, Kelly got his wish when Lurie re-assigned Roseman out of the personnel department (he still did salary-cap business), but the team was lost.

It was around that same time that Douglas was too.

I was in a dark place. I really was. I was about to make good on my promise to beat (Smith's) ass. I sat there for six months and the only reason I didn't go up there and beat his ass was I didn't want my kids to see me in jail. It would have been worth my while. I would have gone to jail for good reason. But I didn't want my kids to see me in jail. And believe me I would have been in jail.

I was nuclear. I was toxic, super toxic. I sat home for two years. People thought I put my hands on him or called him something. And I didn't do any of that. So I just sat around for two years. Until I got a job at 92.9 The Game in Atlanta.

CHAPTER 20

LOVING ATLANTA

To be successful in two major markets, Philly and Atlanta, Jemele Hill and Michael Smith can both kiss my Black ass. I've proven both of them wrong. I survived and thrived in two major markets, two totally different markets.

After sitting around for two years after his departure from ESPN, Douglas found new life in his adopted hometown of Atlanta and on 92.9 The Game.

I was living in Atlanta and my wife, Simona, told me (former Pittsburgh Steelers quarterback) Kordell Stewart was leaving 92.9 The Game. and how that might be an opportunity for me.

Now who do I know at 92.9? I didn't think I knew anybody who was there. Then I remembered (former Atlanta Falcons running back) Jamal Anderson did some work there. I called him and I asked him if he had any contacts and he said Sean Thompson, the program director. I sent Thompson an email, told him who I was and what I was interested in doing. As it turned out he was a Jets fan growing up and remembered me playing for them. And he answered my email. We got to talking. I told him I would like an opportunity and yada, yada, yada.

Another old friend from ESPN helped as well. Not everyone at ESPN was a hater.

Terry Fox was at 92.9, I think he was the general manager, and Terry had a great track record in radio. He was also friends with Stephen A. Smith. I texted Stephen A. and asked him if he could get me a sit down with Terry. That I just needed to get my foot in the door. And could he help me?

I don't like asking people for anything, but I needed an alley-oop. You should only call in favors when you absolutely need one. And I needed one. Stephen A. called and vouched for me. But he also told me, "Hey, Hugh, don't go down there and fuck this up." He said it just like that. I got the meeting with Terry and Stephen had given him the story. I remember Terry said most athletes don't want to work hard, don't want to put in the time, don't want to do certain things because it's too hard.

I told him I don't have that problem. Give me the opportunity and I'll take advantage of it.

Just as the NFL was about to kick off the 2015 season with training camps about to open across the league, the call came and a new window was about to open.

Right before Falcons training camp started, like three days before, I got a call. Sean called me. They put me on the Falcons training camp coverage. I did that every day. And everything else they asked me to do, I did. If they would have asked me to clean the toilets I would have cleaned the toilets. That's just where I was. I'm leaving ESPN where I have these people saying I don't have a work ethic and I know that's not true. But that was the light they were trying to paint me. So I worked my way up the ranks. When there was a show that needed to be filled, I filled in, like every shift. It didn't matter to me. I worked hard. I needed to clear my name.

It began with the live shows from the Falcons training camp, co-hosting with Anderson and Chuck Smith. That led to doing the Falcons pregame show every week, and any show where a host was needed.

I worked with everyone and I didn't care. I just wanted to work. I would have worked with Bozo the Clown if they wanted me to do that. I got the opportunity and I seized it.

Just as he did as that undersized, small-school defensive end who became a three-time Pro Bowl player. It was a different chip that sat on his shoulder this time. But the result was the same.

I didn't like the way I was being portrayed. Is my method or style unorthodox? Okay, that's fine. But who are you to say I don't work hard? Just because I don't take notes like you do. I was there for a reason. And I was good enough or I wouldn't have been there. So now I'm trying to work my way back into the good graces with everyone.

Atlanta radio is different than Philadelphia radio. Probably most everywhere radio is different than Philadelphia radio. So for Douglas it was another change, another challenge.

There's a lot of college football talk. So I was behind the eight ball on two fronts. I didn't play in Atlanta. And I did not go to a SEC school.

Philly radio is also more caller driven. In Atlanta it was more conversational. We took calls now and then, but not like in Philly. We had coaches and players come on with us all the time. It was just a different style of radio. But I enjoyed it. I really did. I loved my time in Atlanta.

As Douglas began a new career in a new city, the Eagles were starting over again as well with a rookie head coach in their one-time, one-year quarterback Doug Pederson and a rookie quarterback in Carson Wentz, the No. 2 overall pick in the 2016 NFL Draft.

Roseman, now back in charge after Chip Kelly was let go, had a busy offseason. Not only did he have to hire a new head coach—and all roads led to New York Giants offensive coordinator Ben McAdoo until the Giants promoted him—he also traded three different players—linebacker Kiko Alonso, running back DeMarco Murray and cornerback Byron Maxwell and six draft picks.

The Eagles were slotted with the 13th pick of the 2016 Draft after finishing Kelly's final year with the team 7–9. Roseman's first move was to trade with the Miami Dolphins, using Alonso, Maxwell, and pick 13 to get the Dolphins No. 8 overall pick. Then he used No. 8, along with a third and a fourth-round pick (acquired from Tennessee for Murray) as well as a 2017 first-round pick and a 2018 second-round pick, to move up with the Cleveland Browns for the No. 2 pick.

With that pick the Eagles selected Wentz out of North Dakota State.

The plan was for the rookie quarterback to sit and watch behind veteran starter Sam Bradford and veteran backup Chase Daniel, who came with Pederson from Kansas City. It was the same plan that worked so well back in 1999 when the Eagles selected Donovan McNabb with that same No. 2 overall pick. Pederson knew that strategy very well since he was the veteran who kept the seat warm for McNabb in 1999. That changed late in preseason when the Minnesota Vikings lost starting quarterback Teddy Bridgewater to an awful knee injury. Roseman shipped Bradford to the Vikings and got a 2017 first-round pick back in the deal. The team saw enough of Daniel in the preseason games to go with the rookie Wentz as their starter.

Wentz and Pederson began their rookie seasons with three straight wins over Cleveland, Chicago and a blowout 34–3 win over Pittsburgh. In those wins, Wentz threw for 769 yards with five touchdowns and no interceptions. In his first four games Wentz had a QB rating of 100, or greater, three times. But he never topped that mark again the rest of the season.

A one-point loss to Detroit a week after their Week 4 bye, sent the Eagles off to lose four of five games And then after a win over eventual NFC champion Atlanta, five more losses made the team 5–9 before they closed with two wins over division rivals New York and Dallas. Those two wins to end the season in Pederson's first year as coach was eerily similar to 1999 when the Eagles won the last two games of Andy Reid's rookie season.

Douglas' first year in Atlanta went a little differently. It started a little slow, but got better and better as the city grew fond of its adopted son.

When I first started working (in Atlanta), people knew I played in the NFL, knew I played for the Eagles. And that the Falcons lost to the Eagles in the playoffs. And there were people who wanted me off the air. I would tell people to kiss my ass. I played in Philly and worked radio in Philly. I could handle them.

Terry called me in the office and told me, "Hugh, you can't say stuff like that."

I said, "Well they can't say what they say to me."

He said, "You have to be above that."

I said. "I'm not above that. I'm not."

After a while I would try to be more crafty, more slick. I would thank them for listening and all of that. Then we started doing pretty good. It took them a while, but I have to say what I will always respect about the people of Atlanta was they embraced me like I was one of them. And to this day I still get people down there telling me they miss me.

In that first year in Atlanta, Douglas and Co. were getting ready for the Falcons to go to just their second ever Super Bowl. They could never be ready for what happened in the game.

It was bananas. This is not a slight. The fans came out and showed out. But it's not like Philly. But those Dirty Bird fans showed out.

It's just different. In Atlanta the party was outside. When I first got there I went to a tailgate with these people called HellGaters. Their tailgate was so lit. They would have concerts from local artists who would perform at the tailgate. You know how most places, like Philly, when the game starts everyone goes into the game, right? People in Atlanta listened to the concert first, then went into the game. It was just different.

What I remember most about the Super Bowl year was the year before they went to the Super Bowl people there used to talk bad about (quarterback) Matt Ryan. They probably still do. I would get heat because I would tell them, "You're going to miss Matt Ryan when he's gone. Matt Ryan is a Hall of Famer." They told me I was crazy.

Ryan took the Falcons to that Super Bowl LI and had a 28–3 lead over Tom Brady and the New England Patriots in the third quarter. You know what happened next.

Even though 28–3 will live in infamy, Matt Ryan is probably the best quarterback in Falcons history. But he doesn't get that love, because he's White and he was coming off the heels of Michael Vick.

Of course to all the fans, It was Matt Ryan's fault (the Falcons blew the 28–3 lead and lost in overtime, 34–28). I was like, no, it was the defense's fault. They were like, we didn't score. I said they scored enough points to win the game. Sure they could have scored more. But they scored 28 against that New England defense.

I watched that game with my son Hugh and he was like, "The Falcons about to win the Super Bowl." I told him there's a lot of time left on the clock. And I'll be damned. It was still Tom Brady.

As of 2025, the Falcons have never gone back to the Super Bowl. Douglas did get to see the Braves win the World Series in 2021. And, of course there's the No. 1 sports team in Atlanta—the University of Georgia Bulldogs football.

I remember Sean telling me make sure you keep up with the Braves, know what they're doing. Even though our station didn't carry the Braves games we still talked about them. And he told me you really have to stay on top of Georgia football.

Loved being in Atlanta, loved it, I just loved being in Atlanta. It was just a great city for me. I loved the time I was there. I love the way they embraced me. Atlanta owes me nothing. They didn't want me to leave.

A lot of people helped me get back on my feet in Atlanta. People say to me, "You love Atlanta." I can't not love Atlanta. They gave me a place to stay when I didn't have anywhere to go.

To be fired and to be as toxic as I was and to be there for almost 10 years and they didn't want me to leave, I think that says something.

Another thing happened while Douglas was in Atlanta: the Eagles won their first Super Bowl.

I told my boss, and Terry is a Cowboys fan by the way. When the Eagles won the Super Bowl I told Terry I need this day off because the Eagles won the Super Bowl and I'm going to the parade.

Hugh and I jumped in the car and we went to the parade. On the way there I got pulled over in Carolina. I was really getting it. I told the police officer the Eagles won the Super Bowl and we're going to the parade. He said, "Okay, but just slow it down."

CHAPTER 21

NICK FOLES, DOUG PEDERSON, AND SUPER BOWL LII

We got to the Eagles parade in the morning and all the people were already out there. It was an amazing scene. But it was great to see. I was happy for the team. I mean, it was bananas. Jason Kelce's speech wearing the Mummer's outfit. It was some scene. But you kind of knew it would be. That's why I wanted to go.

Some, if not most, Eagles fans had waited their entire lives for a championship. Not since 1960, when Chuck Bednarik tackled Green Bay's Jim Taylor as the final seconds ticked off the clock, had the Eagles been NFL champions, much less Super Bowl Champions. As far as Super Bowls were concerned, the Eagles were 0-for-51.

Until February 4, 2018.

Winning a championship and what it means to the city of Philadelphia is something else. It just means more here. I mean the last one before (the Eagles Super Bowl win) was the Phillies winning the World Series (in 2008 and before that the 76ers in 1983). Nothing against the Phillies, but Philadelphia is a football city and people love the Eagles.

There was no indication that the 2017 Eagles with second-year head coach Doug Pederson and second-year quarterback Carson Wentz would end that drought of no championships. The team went 7–9 in both men's rookie seasons, but went 4–9 in their last 13 games. There were a few subtle changes to the roster, adding wide receiver Alshon Jeffery for one, but nothing drastic. They didn't go out and sign a Ricky Watters type free agent or trade for a Terrell Owens. Instead, it was a young quarterback with a young head coach hoping to take the team back to the playoffs for the first time since 2013 and to maybe win a playoff game for the first time since 2008. They did so much more.

They had a good, balanced team. Offensively they ran the ball well and (Wentz) made plays in the passing game. Defense, they were very solid and very fundamentally sound. And then they got hot.

The Eagles won the 2017 opener against Washington, 30–17, as Wentz threw for 307 yards and two first-half touchdowns. The defense held

Washington to 264 total yards and forced four turnovers, one a fumble return for a touchdown by defensive tackle Fletcher Cox.

In Week 2, as is usually the case, the mentor beat the mentee as Pederson's Eagles lost to Andy Reid and the Kansas City Chiefs, 27–20. They wouldn't lose again for another 76 days. The Eagles went into their midseason bye week, 8–1 and were 10–1 before they lost to the Seahawks in Seattle. It was the week after that Seattle game where the season could have come apart, but instead was defined.

In a 43–35 shootout win over the Rams in Los Angeles, the Eagles moved to 11–2 and clinched the NFC East and top seed in the NFC for the playoffs. They also lost Wentz, who was having an MVP caliber season, to a season-ending knee injury. Longtime Eagles fans were as stunned as they were frustrated and heart broken. This was going to be the year and now their MVP was finished.

Enter Nick Foles.

Folk hero, that's what he was.

Foles had one of the most unique careers of anyone who has ever played in the NFL. With the Eagles he looked like Joe Montana or Tom Brady, with anyone else he looked like Hannah Montana or Marcia Brady. His first extended playing time with the Eagles came in 2013 under Chip Kelly and he threw for 27 touchdowns with just two interceptions. Included in that was an NFL record-tying seven touchdown game against the Raiders in Oakland.

After an injury-plagued 2014 season, Kelly traded Foles to the Rams. He started 11 games for Los Angeles, threw more interceptions than touchdowns (10–7), and with the team 4–7 was benched. He played a year in Kansas City as Alex Smith's backup for Reid, who took him in the third round of the 2012 NFL Draft, and then came back to the Eagles. Folk-hero status aside. He came back as Wentz' backup and after his Super Bowl heroics left for a big contract with Jacksonville in 2019. He started four games for the Jaguars and the team lost all four. Things weren't any better in Chicago in 2020 and 2021, or in

Indianapolis with his Eagles offensive coordinator Frank Reich, then the Colts head coach, in 2022.

Not counting his rookie year of 2012, Foles won 20 of 26 starts with the Eagles. He won just eight of 26 starts with the Rams, Chiefs, Jaguars, Bears, and Colts.

Nick played to his strengths and played to the strengths of the players around him. That's how he succeeded. You marry your quarterback to the skills of the players you have.

Foles took over for Wentz with three games left in the regular season. He threw four touchdowns in a 34–29 win over the two-win Giants. But was shaky in a 19–10 win over the Raiders and played just a half, a bad half, in a 6–0 loss in a meaningless last game of the season to the Cowboys.

Then came the playoffs.

Nick was a little rocky that first (playoff) game. Then he got comfortable. What Nick thrived at was he got the ball out quickly and into the hands of the playmakers.

That first playoff game, after a first-round bye, was against the defending NFC champion Atlanta Falcons. Despite the Eagles being the top seed and at home, the Falcons, off a wild-card win over the Rams, were a slight favorite. Not everyone, even some in Atlanta, thought the Falcons were a lock, however.

I was nervous being in Atlanta. People were mad at me, of course, because I said I thought the Eagles were going to win. And they wanted me out of town again. But I just call it as I see it. And I didn't see the Falcons going to Philly and beating the Eagles.

It wasn't easy. The Eagles used a fortunate bounce before the half and a tough goal-line stand at the end of the game to beat the Falcons, 15–10, With Atlanta ahead, 10–6, the Eagles faced second-and-8 from their 30-yard line with 22 seconds left in the first half. Foles threw what looked like an interception that would have set up the Falcons for a field goal to increase their lead. Instead the ball bounced off the Falcons defender and into the hands of wide receiver Torrey Smith, who brought it to midfield. A 15-yard completion to Jeffery got the Eagles to the Falcons 35-yard line and Jake Elliott hit a 53-yard field goal to close the gap to 10–9.

Two more Elliott field goal made it 15–10, but the Falcons drove to a first-and-goal at the Eagles' 9-yard line with 1:19 left on the clock. Matt Ryan threw incomplete on first and second down. Falcons wide receiver Julio Jones, who finished with nine receptions for 101 yards, got the Falcons to the 2-yard line with a seven-yard catch. On fourth-and-2, Ryan went back to Jones, but threw too high and the Eagles held on. They were in the NFC title game, where they would host the NFC North champion Minnesota Vikings.

Minnesota, which beat New Orleans in a game that became known as "The Minneapolis Miracle" in the conference semifinals, was not a challenge. Foles threw for 352 yards and three touchdowns and the Eagles blew out the Vikings, 38–7. That meant a trip to Super Bowl LII in Minnesota and a meeting with Tom Brady and the New England Patriots.

I thought it would be a tough game. But I felt in my heart the Eagles had a chance. When it came down to the last waning minutes of the game it got a little nerve wracking, but they came through.

Was it hard not being in Philly? Not really. Remember, I was starting over in Atlanta after what happened (at ESPN). So I was still getting my feet wet there. It was all good. I did stay in touch with some guys back there. I talked to Ike (Reese, former teammate and now a radio host on WIP) periodically. So I knew what was going on up there. And we were all happy for the team.

Super Bowl LII proved to be one of the most exciting Super Bowls ever played. The Eagles and Foles outlasted Brady and the Patriots, 41–33, to win the franchise's first-ever Super Bowl after losing Super Bowls XV and XXXIX. New England gained 613 yards, never punted, and was 6-for-12 on third and fourth down conversions. And lost. The Eagles gained 538 yards and were 12-for-18 on third and fourth down conversions.

Foles threw for 373 yards and three touchdowns. Veteran running back LeGarrette Blount ran for 90 yards. Rookie running back Corey Clement caught four passes for 100 yards and wide receiver Nelson Agholor—a first-round pick thought to be a bust at times—had nine catches for 84 yards.

Brady threw for 505 yards and three touchdowns and had three 100-plus-yard receivers in Danny Amendola, Chris Hogan, and Rob Gronkowski.

Foles also caught a touchdown pass on what might be the gutsiest play call in Super Bowl history. With 34 seconds left in the first half, the Eagles led, 15–12, and faced fourth-and-goal from the New England 1-yard line. Pederson called time out and when Foles came to the sideline he told his coach, "Let's go Philly, Philly." The real name of the play was Philly Special.

Pederson told his quarterback, "Yeah, let's go for it."

On the play, Foles lined up in shotgun formation, but just before the snap he moved to his right. The ball was snapped directly to Clement, an undrafted rookie, who went left and then pitched the ball to No. 3 tight end Trey Burton, who threw to a wide-open Foles in the end zone for a touchdown.

That was phenomenal. Would Andy have ever called that? Hell no. But hey that was Doug. And at that point you're playing with house money, so why not?

Pederson took those kinds of chances all season and more times than not they paid off for him. The life-time backup quarterback and basically unknown assistant coach under Andy Reid, had done what no-one else had ever done at the time—he won a Super Bowl with the Philadelphia Eagles.

Sure I remember Doug. He was the bridge quarterback for Donovan (McNabb). All we knew about him when he got there was he was Brett Favre's backup (in Green Bay). And he was Brett Favre's best friend. And Andy brought him (to Philadelphia) to be that bridge.

Doug knew what he was signing up for when he came to the Eagles. I'm sure Andy briefed him at how tough it was going to be. I mean let's be honest Doug wasn't that good (of a quarterback). He was a backup. That's what he was. But Doug was smart. That's what made him a smart coach. He knew coming here he was going to get all the slings and arrows in order for Donovan to come up and do what he did. But Doug did what he was supposed to do and got paid for it.

As a coach he was Andy's protégé. I thought it was (a good hire) because he played for the Eagles so he knew the city. He knew what to expect. He knew what it was like there. He had been working with Andy, so I figured—let's give him a chance. Maybe he learned from Andy's mistakes. Andy learned from his mistakes in Philly when he got to Kansas City. He wasn't the same coach he was in Philly. And he learned from the mistakes he made, so maybe Doug did too.

Pederson and Foles are legends in Philadelphia. They even put up a statue of them conferring on the "Philly Special" outside of Lincoln Financial Field.

Nick became the greatest quarterback in Eagles history according to some, because he won the Super Bowl. But before the playoffs started there was a lot of trepidation about Nick. Now, you can't say anything bad about Nick. I said once that if I'm looking back over Eagles quarterbacks I would take Mike Vick over Nick Foles. People went apeshit over that.

And what about the quarterback who led the Eagles to the No. 1 seed, the one who was going to be league MVP before the knee injury? As it turned out his career was never the same after Super Bowl LII. Wentz threw for 3,296 yards and 33 touchdowns in the 13 games he played in 2017 and the Eagles were 11–2. He had his moments in 2019 and 2020, but after being traded to the Colts in 2021 he played for Washington (in 2022), Los Angeles (in 2023), and Kansas City (in 2024), and Minnesota (in 2025).

Carson Wentz, you know what's funny? I would hear stuff when I would go up (to Philly) to visit. Now I never met Carson personally, but people in the organization when I would mention him, or say his name, there was almost a gag order. From what I heard, Carson was not a good dude. That's what I gathered from the people there. Like Jalen (Hurts) is quirky, but I never heard anyone say he was a bad person. I never heard anyone say Donovan was a bad person. But from my perspective, when I brought up Carson's name nobody wanted to talk about him. To me that was a red flag. Then he gets hurt and Nick Foles takes over and you really started hearing stuff happening behind the scenes.

And, hey, some of it that is natural. Your backup won the Super Bowl. You got hurt, but you won the Super Bowl. That's not easy. And then when you really started hearing about Carson is when they drafted Jalen. Then the shit really hit the fan. His fall from grace fell hard. Part of that was a little karma. He just never bounced back from all of that.

Hey, quarterbacks are built different. Those cats, they want to be team guys, but they're individuals more than anything. They are treated differently. They're the only ones who have the coach's direct number. They're the only ones for the most part who go to the coach's office every week. They're the only ones who are not allowed to get hit at practice. They're coddled from the time they start playing quarterback all the way to the time they make it in the pros. They're just treated different. And it is what it is.

Back to Super Bowl LII.

The Eagles took a 38–33 lead when Foles found tight end Zach Ertz for an 11-yard touchdown with 2:21 to play. But a five-point deficit with over two minutes is nothing to Brady and the Pats. Just ask the Falcons.

Brady found Gronk for eight yards on first down and it was second-and-2 from the 33-yard line. Brandon Graham, a first-round pick of the Eagles back in 2010, had finally emerged as one of the team's top pass rushers. He then made the play of his career and one of the most important in Eagles history. Graham beat his man, sacked Brady, and stripped the ball loose. Derrick Barnett recovered and it led to an Elliott field goal and a 41–33 lead with a minute to play.

Brandon was one of the few guys I knew on that team, because I had met him when I was still in Philly. Then he had that strip sack and that play put him in a different light. BG is blessed. A lot of guys in his position, they don't stick and stay the way he did. Courtney Brown was a No.

1 overall pick (of the Cleveland Browns in 2000). In five years he had 17 sacks and he was done, as the first overall pick. (Brown played one more year with Denver and got another two sacks). He was done. Brandon Graham in his first five years had 17 sacks. And played 11 more years all with the Eagles. Brandon tells the story how after one game him and Howie (Eagles GM Roseman) had a moment. And Howie told him, "If you don't succeed, I don't succeed." And for Brandon to be here as long as he was, that just doesn't happen.

He was able to stay and thrive. It didn't matter if he had different defensive coordinators, because he was a smart player. I admire BG. Because these fans hated him when he started here. They thought he was a bust. And you know how nasty it can get in Philly. He told me he would go home and him and his wife would pray about it. Now today, you see him out and he speaks to everybody, he's kind to everybody. If it was me I'd be, "Fuck y'all. You the same ones who talked bad about me." He doesn't do that. And I admire that. I really do.

Pederson, Foles, Graham, and even Wentz were all major story lines for that first-ever Eagles Super Bowl win. But it goes back a little further.

Coming back and being a part of it and seeing the people in the streets going wild, yeah I was a little envious. But I was happy for them. I really was. I know on some level we kind of got it started. Now we don't get the same adulation they get because we didn't win it, but we were part of the foundation that laid the groundwork for the Eagles to be in the position they were in then. And for that I'm forever grateful.

CHAPTER 22

FROM DOUG TO NICK AND CARSON TO JALEN

There was a difference of opinion. Doug didn't want to be a puppet. You know Howie Roseman runs the team. Howie is that dude. He picks the pieces. He puts it altogether.

You would think the head coach that won the Eagles first Super Bowl and won it his way would be the head coach for as long as he wanted. You might also think the quarterback the team traded a bunch of players and picks to acquire and then gave a huge new contract would also be around for a while.

Not in Philadelphia.

Doug Pederson won the Eagles first-ever Super Bowl in 2017, made the playoffs in 2018 and 2019 and was gone after a forgettable 4–11–1 2020 season.

Carson Wentz, who was on his way to a MVP award in 2017 before tearing his ACL, was injured again in 2018, knocked out of the playoff game with a concussion in 2019, benched in 2020 and traded before the 2021 season.

From the outside looking in, Doug's firing felt like it had something to do with Carson at first. They drafted Jalen. Carson wasn't happy. And shortly after that they moved on from Doug. Then come to find out Doug wrote a book and said in it him and Jeff Lurie fell out about the direction of the team basically. It was unfortunate that that was the case. Doug comes in, a relative unknown, has a ballsy way to win the Super Bowl. And then he's gone.

Pederson never had much say in personnel matters or even his coaching staff in his five years as head coach of the Eagles. Roseman not only picked the 53-man roster (as a lot of general managers do), he also decided who was active on game days. It was also telling that the team hired defensive coordinator Jim Schwartz before it hired Pederson in 2016. And for a first-time head coach that was okay. After winning a Super Bowl, the head coach wanted more say at least when it came to his staff. That wasn't going to be the case. So after a lengthy discussion on who his coordinators would be before the 2021 season, Pederson and the Eagles decided to part ways.

So now enter Nick Sirianni. I didn't like him at first. You know every job interview I ever had I got dressed up for it. I put some nice clothes on for it. When he interviewed for the Eagles' job it came off a little arrogant to me. He was on vacation and they had to meet him wherever he was and dress down for him.

Actually, Sirianni and his family were on vacation in Florida and the Eagles interviewed him at Lurie's house in Palm Beach. They conducted other interviews there as well that year.

Then he has his press conference and he sounds like a bubblehead. But I'll tell you what, with all that being said and since I've been back here, Nick is a perfect fit for Philadelphia. I still call him "Coach Bubblehead," but he's perfect for Philadelphia. He really is.

Sirianni is a different breed of NFL head coach. His early press conferences bordered on the bizarre. He was killed in the media for his initial press conference, even though it was conducted via Zoom where he was alone in the Eagles auditorium, with the reporters at their homes. He uses analytics to the utmost and goes for it on fourth down even more than Pederson did. He makes old time fans scratch and shake their heads when they're not getting in screaming matches with him during and after games. When the team stumbled home after a 10–1 start in 2023 to finish 11–7 and out of the playoffs in the first round, there was actual talk of his firing. Fans wanted him gone. Some in the media, both local and national, wanted him gone. Even some in the organization wanted him gone. One of the few who didn't want him gone, was the only one who counted—Jeffrey Lurie. Sirianni rewarded his boss with a Super Bowl title in 2024.

When they went on that run (in 2024), he shaved his head. When you do something that drastic, and I've heard people say this, when you have something drastic happen, you change your hair. It's like a reset. I remember doing the pregame show that week and we heard Nick cut his hair and first thing that came to my mind was, "Oh they about to go on a run. This might be historic." My partner (on the radio) Joe Giglio thought I was crazy.

The run went all the way to the Super Bowl and a blowout of the trying-to-three-peat Kansas City Chiefs. Sirianni, the unknown coach replacing the man who won a Super Bowl, now had one of his own. What the coach has done best, besides coach, is get along with both his players and his boss. Roseman, the GM, had had a difficult time getting along with his head coaches. Andy Reid tolerated him. Chip Kelly hated him. Pederson had the falling out. Roseman and Sirianni seem to get along just fine and their success speaks to that fact.

I didn't know much about him. All I knew about him was he played at Mount Union. He was a wide receiver. Coached in Indianapolis. An offensive guy, I really didn't know a whole lot. Since he's been here, and for whatever reason, he's had his finger on the pulse of this team. Which goes to show you never judge a book by its cover.

I like the way he does it, too. He sent a big FU to anyone who didn't believe in him. I mean going to two Super Bowls in his first four years. That's pretty impressive. In a performance based business for you to do that, that's impressive.

He's different, but it's a different NFL. You can't put players in a box and treat them the way coaches like Bill Parcells did back in the day. You can't do that. It's not going to work. Nick Sirianni related to the guys on a level like no other. You talk about the social media part of it and the fact that he's fairly young and he understands that. I feel like in order to get through to some guys in this day and age you have to see them at their level. And he does that.

Listen, Philadelphia is a tough place, there's no question about that. And we're super critical of the players and coaches. It is what it is. And when coach got into those battles, and people questioning him, and is he the right guy for the job, and should he be fired, the players related to that. And that's because they deal with all that kind of stuff as well.

When Sirianni was hired to replace Pederson, Wentz was still the quarterback. The outside thought from those in the know was Wentz may have been one of, if not the main, reason why Pederson left. A new head coach with a different offensive approach may make all the difference for the franchise quarterback. So much for that theory. Wentz was traded to the Indianapolis Colts 24 days after the team hired their new coach. Sirianni was the Eagles head coach and Jalen Hurts, selected in the second round of the 2020 Draft, was the Eagles quarterback. At least going into the 2021 season that was the plan.

My first thought (when the Eagles drafted Hurts) was, "Oh shit, Carson is going to be mad." You're talking about a guy who didn't get the accolades. He got the Eagles to where they could get to the Super Bowl, but he never got the accolades because he got hurt. Then they pay you but then they draft a quarterback. The thing was, and this hurt him, he didn't embrace the competition. He said, "I'm out." And he has never been the same since.

Pederson sat out the 2021 season and resurfaced in Jacksonville, where he took the Jaguars to the AFC South title and a playoff win in 2022. A late-season collapse in 2023 followed by a 4–13 season in 2024 cost him his job. Wentz bounced from Indianapolis to Washington to back-up roles in Los Angeles, Kansas City, and Minnesota.

Sirianni and Hurts made the playoffs in 2021 as a 9–8 wild-card team that won the tiebreaker over the New Orleans Saints thanks to a head-to-head win. They were knocked out in the first round by Tom Brady and Tampa Bay, 31–15, in a game not as close as the score might say it was.

During that 2022 offseason, two big-name quarterbacks were about to be traded. Houston was looking to move DeShaun Watson, who was dealing with off-the-field troubles. And Seattle was offering Super Bowl winner Russell Wilson to anyone who would make it a good offer. The Eagles were interested in both. Neither was interested in Philadelphia. So the Eagles didn't get either one. But it wasn't for a lack of trying. Watson ended up in Cleveland in exchange for three first-round draft picks, a third-round pick and two fourth-round picks. Wilson went to Denver in exchange for two first-round picks, two second-round picks, a fifth-round pick, and three players, including quarterback Drew Lock.

And the Eagles stuck with Hurts.

What do they say? You would rather be lucky than good. The Eagles were lucky there.

All Hurts has done since no trade was made is take the Eagles to two Super Bowls, losing a tough game to Kansas City in Super Bowl LVII and beating the Chiefs two years later in Super Bowl LIX, where he was named the game's Most Valuable Player. Watson has been nothing but hurt in Cleveland and Wilson bounced from Denver to Pittsburgh to the New York Giants in the span of three years.

They say his numbers aren't pretty. But one thing about Jalen and this goes back to him in college. The one thing he's always had is unquantifiable intangibles. Everything we talk about when we talk about quarterbacks has to be based on something tangible. The stats, the passer rating, the QBR, all of that. This guy just goes out and wins any way he can. When I tell people that and how good he is. They say this and that and what about his stats.

They talk about (Baltimore's) Lamar Jackson and (Cincinnati's) Joe Burrow and (Buffalo's) Josh Allen, when you put together Jalen's résumé compared to those other guys—not the stats, the résumé—it's all Jalen. The stats may favor those other guys, but Jalen's résumé is impeccable. If you're hiring a guy for a job, now I'm not talking stats, not talking completion percentage, yards, ratings any of that, I'm talking about résumé. He has one hell of a résumé.

We've gone so far one way when it comes to ranking quarterbacks, and what makes a good quarterback. All I know is this MF wins games. Don't tell me about the labor pains, show me the baby. People talk about the regular season and they say the playoffs are different. Well, he took all the arrows that were slung at him and did what he had to do during the regular season. And he stepped it up in the playoffs, and came out the other side as a Super Bowl champion and MVP. Show me the baby.

Sirianni and Hurts share a lot of similar traits. They both grew up in football households where their fathers were coaches. They both love the game. Where the differences occur is while Sirianni is criticized for how he responds in press conferences and how he acts on the sidelines, at times showing too much emotion, Hurts is the opposite. He's somewhat emotionless, at least publicly.

Jalen doesn't run hot and cold. He's just Jalen. He doesn't say anything. He doesn't talk about being hurt. He doesn't talk about playing bad. He doesn't talk about playing good. He just doesn't talk about anything. He's reserved. He just goes out there and gets the job done. He does what's needed in the moment.

CHAPTER 23

THE EAGLES HALL OF FAME

You know I messed it up right? I was on the air in Atlanta. Dave Spadaro (of the Eagles) called me. Jeffrey Lurie came on the phone and told me, "Congratulations, you're going into the Eagles Hall of Fame." I announced it (on the radio) the day they told me. But I wasn't supposed to say anything. I was supposed to wait until the Eagles announced it.

I remember later Dave said, "In true Hugh Douglas form, he told everyone when he wasn't supposed to tell anyone." But I was just so excited about it. It was a big deal for me. But yeah, I screwed it up. But I was on brand, for anyone who knows me I was on brand. Doing shit out of turn.

The call came early in the 2022 NFL season, a season the Eagles began 8–0 with field goal wins over Detroit and Arizona and blowout wins over Minnesota, Washington and Pittsburgh. Douglas and a fellow defensive end, Trent Cole, were going to be inducted into the Philadelphia Eagles Hall of Fame when the team hosted the Green Bay Packers, November 27 on Sunday Night Football.

It was really exciting. I got fitted for the jacket and everything. The great part about it for me was my sons, Hugh and Harper, were there. Hugh came up and hung out for a little while, but he had to go back to take a test for school. He couldn't miss the test. But he was there for most of it. The only bad part was my daughters (Kayla and Brianna) couldn't make it. But it was a great time. It was great to be a part of it. To hear that "Huuuuuuugh" chant one last time. It was all great.

The Eagles organization likes to do things with a rhyme to their reason, so it was not a coincidence that when the committee that decides on the Hall inductees got together that Douglas and Cole were inducted into the Hall the same year. Cole was the team's fifth-round draft pick out of Cincinnati in 2005. Douglas' last year with the team as a player was 2004. They were basically the same kind of player, too: tough, quick pass rushers from the right defensive end position. Douglas played 10 years in the league, six with the

Eagles, and finished with 80 sacks (54½ with the Eagles). That's an average of eight sacks per season and nine sacks per season as an Eagle. Cole played 12 years in the league, 10 with the Eagles, and finished with 90 1/2 sacks (85½ with the Eagles). That's an average of 7½ sacks per season and 8½ per season as an Eagle. It goes even further than that.

I always said that Trent was my protégé in a way. I played at Central State (in Ohio) and he was from Xenia (Ohio). He used to come to some of my practices when he was younger. So it was only fitting that we went in together.

As of the end of the 2025 season, there were 52 players and two championship teams—the back to back 1948 and 1949 NFL Champions—in the Eagles Hall of Fame. Only four of those 52 players were defensive ends—Reggie White, Clyde Simmons, Hugh Douglas, and Trent Cole. Brandon Graham, who retired after the 2024 season, is sure to make it five. But for now there are just four.

Here's the complete list of the players inducted into the Eagles Hall in alphabetical order:

David Akers, Kicker

Eric Allen, Cornerback

Maxie Baughan, Linebacker

Chuck Bednarik, Center/Linebacker

Bert Bell, Owner/Head Coach

Bill Bergey, Linebacker

Bill Bradley, Safety

Tom Brookshier, Cornerback

Bob Brown, Tackle

Jerome Brown, Defensive Tackle

Tim Brown, Running Back

Leo Carlin, Administration

Harold Carmichael, Wide receiver

Trent Cole, Defensive End

Randall Cunningham, Quarterback
Otho Davis, Trainer
Brian Dawkins, Safety
Hugh Douglas, Defensive End
Jimmy Gallagher, Administration
Bill Hewitt, Receiver
Ron Jaworski, Quarterback
Malcolm Jenkins, Safety
Jim Johnson, Defensive Coordinator
Seth Joyner, Linebacker
Sonny Jurgensen, Quarterback
Bucko Kilroy, Defensive Tackle
Ollie Matson, Running Back
LeSean McCoy, Running Back
Tommy McDonald, Wide Receiver
Donovan McNabb, Quarterback
Wilbert Montgomery, Running Back
Earl "Greasy" Neale, Head Coach
Pete Pihos, Receiver
Mike Quick, Wide Receiver
Merrill Reese, Announcer
Pete Retzlaff, Tight End
Jim Ringo, Center
Jon Runyan, Tackle
Clyde Simmons, Defensive End
Jerry Sisemore, Tackle
Tra Thomas, Tackle
Jeremiah Trotter, Linebacker
Norm Van Brocklin, Quarterback
Steve Van Buren, Running Back
Dick Vermeil, Head Coach

Troy Vincent, Cornerback
Stan Walters, Tackle
Bobby Walston, Receiver
Brian Westbrook, Running Back
Reggie White, Defensive End
Al Wistert, Tackle
Alex Wojeiechowicz, Center

The Eagles have been around since 1933, so to be one of 52 players selected and inducted into their Hall of Fame is quite the accomplishment. And to be one of just four at your position makes it even more amazing.

I never thought about it like that. You put it in perspective when you say that. But I never thought about that. It's humbling. It never dawned on me. But it's something, especially from a team that didn't draft me, to end up in their Hall of Fame. The Eagles didn't draft me. And to have that kind of honor and in a city like Philadelphia, it's an awesome feeling. And you think about the company you're in and the fact that I'm in with those guys that's pretty impressive.

Especially when one of the players at your position is Reggie White, one of the greatest players in the history of the game. White, a Pro Football Hall of Famer, is one of only a handful of players to be inducted into the Hall of Fame of two teams, the Eagles and the Green Bay Packers.

Reggie is the Hallmark. I grew up watching Reggie White and (Buffalo's) Bruce Smith. I read all about Bruce Smith's work ethic and all of that. But Reggie was just a freak of nature. His ability to do some of the things he was able to do just set him apart from players at his position. He was a guy when you lined up against him it was going to be a long day, a long ass day. So when you put it like that, yeah (it's really an honor). Because Reggie was a monster.

Eight of the other 51 players in the Eagles Hall and one coach were contemporaries of Douglas—Akers, Dawkins, McNabb, Runyan, Thomas, Trotter, Vincent, Westbrook, and Johnson, his defensive coordinator.

That was a special group of players. I love those guys. I loved playing with them.

Douglas has been inducted into the Black College Hall of Fame and the Central State Hall of Fame as well. Going into the Eagles Hall seemed a little more special.

(Philadelphia is a) passionate city, a real passionate city, especially when it comes to the Eagles. When I think back on all the things I've been through in life the fact that I was in Philadelphia helped me deal with most of it. That never give up mentality, that never quit deal. When I first got to Atlanta I would tell people I played in Philly, so you can't break me. I'm not going to be intimidated. Try again. That's just how I felt.

When Douglas made his announcement, albeit premature, his new town, Atlanta, embraced him as well.

People were congratulating me. Atlanta is a unique place. I love Atlanta. Even though I didn't play there the people in Atlanta were happy for me. Like I've said I got adopted by Atlanta. I have people today from Atlanta that tell me they still listen to me (on the radio in Philadelphia). That says a lot. That's very special for me. That they want to listen to a guy who never played for the team they root for, that's special.

Douglas arrived for his special day the Friday before the Eagles Sunday night game against Green Bay. The team was 9–1 at that point and held a two-game lead over Dallas in the NFC East. The Eagles had already beaten the Cowboys back in Week 6 to hold the tiebreaker advantage as well.

Got there on Friday, had a meet and greet and said a few words. Saturday was a Q&A. Fans came in and asked us questions. We answered the questions and talked a little bit more. It was cool. The kids were there. Trent's family was there. Ike (Reese, Douglas' former teammate) came with his son. It was just a cool vibe to be back in Philly for all of that. And for me it was the first time I had been back to Philly in a while. I had been working in Atlanta and the job I had I never really considered it work because I just run my mouth all day. So I didn't take much time off. I rarely had a vacation.

Sunday was the induction and the Eagles made it a perfect day with a 40–33 shootout win over the Packers. The offense rolled for 500 total yards. Jalen Hurts threw for 153 yards and two touchdowns (to A.J. Brown and Quez Watkins) and ran for 157 yards. Running back Miles Sanders carried 21 times for another 143 yards. The win moved the Eagles to 10–1 on the season and kept them two games ahead of the Cowboys in the NFC East and one game ahead of the NFC North-leading Minnesota Vikings for the top seed in the playoffs.

They were doing well. And that was Jalen's coming out party, if you will. That was a good year for Jalen and a great game. He played the year before and did okay. But (2022) was his first really big year.

Hurts played 15 games that season and the Eagles went 14–1 in those games. They were 0–2 in the two games he missed. The quarterback completed 66.5 percent of his passes, threw for 3,701 yards and had 22 touchdowns to six interceptions. He also ran for 760 yards and another 13 touchdowns. Sanders, the fourth-year running back from Penn State, had a big year as well with 1,269 yards rushing and 11 touchdowns. Brown, acquired in a draft-day trade with the Tennessee Titans, led the receivers with 88 receptions for 1,496 yards and 11 touchdowns. While DeVonta Smith, the first round pick out of Alabama in 2021, had 95 receptions for 1,196 yards and seven touchdowns.

Defensively, safety C.J. Gardner-Johnson had six interceptions to lead the secondary. The pass rush was the key as edge rusher Haasan Reddick had 16 sacks and fellow edges Josh Sweat and Brandon Graham and defensive tackle Javon Hargrave had 11 sacks each.

It was a good, young group of players. It was good to see that and be a part of that. They had a good offense and the defense had a bunch of guys who could get to the quarterback. And then Brandon. He had been there for a while. His longevity was something else. I always admired him for that.

When Minnesota lost to division rivals Detroit and Green Bay it paved the way for the Eagles to get the No. 1 seed in the conference. But first it had to hold off the Cowboys for the NFC East title.

A loss in Dallas, 40–34, moved the Cowboys to within a game of the Eagles, with two to play, but the Eagles closed out the regular season with a 22–16 win over the New York Giants to win the division and earn the No. 1 seed in the playoffs.

In the first round of the postseason, the wild-card Giants upset the Vikings, 31–24, setting up a third game in the divisional round between the two NFC East rivals. You know the old adage about how hard it is to beat a team three times in a season? Don't buy it. Since the AFL/NFL merger there had been 24 occurrences where a team that went 2–0 during the season against an opponent faced that same team in the postseason. The team that went 2–0 was 15–9 in the third game. The Eagles made it 16–9 when they crushed the Giants, 38–7.

Hurts was his efficient self in the win, completing 16 of 24 passes for 154 yards and two touchdowns. Sanders rushed for 90 yards and backup running back Kenneth Gainwell ran for 112. The defense harassed Giants quarterback Daniel Jones all game and sacked him five times. They held Giants running back and their future teammate Saquon Barkley to 61 yards on nine carries. One of those carries was for 39 yards, meaning he had just 22 yards on his other eight carries.

San Francisco and rookie quarterback Brock Purdy beat the Cowboys, 19–12, in the other divisional round game making it a 49ers/Eagles matchup for the NFC title at The Linc.

Purdy, the last player selected in the 2022 NFL Draft, had replaced an injured Jimmy Garoppolo midway through the season and led the 49ers to the NFL title game. It struck midnight for Cinderella late in the first quarter. With the score tied, 7–7, Reddick sacked Purdy, forced a fumble, and sent the quarterback to the sidelines with an elbow injury. Veteran Josh Johnson replaced Purdy but was also knocked out of the game with a concussion in the second half. The Eagles coasted to a 31–7 win and were headed back to the Super Bowl for the second time in six years. Before that they had only been to two Super Bowls in 56 years.

They had a good team, a balanced team. You could tell they were going to do something special.

As special as a kid from Mansfield, Ohio out of tiny Central State who didn't even know if he would get drafted, going into a team's Hall of Fame.

Smallish defensive end, from a small school, who people weren't sure could play (in the NFL), that's not bad. I'll take it. I'll take it all day.

CHAPTER 24

BIG RED VS. THE EAGLES I (SUPER BOWL LVII)

It was a bittersweet thing. Big Red is the one that helped the team have the success in the city they had all those years. He's the one who changed the fortunes for the Eagles. Now he's with the Kansas City Chiefs and he has Patrick Mahomes, the best quarterback in the game, and Andy is coaching him. He has a great coaching staff with him, too. I know a lot of those guys on the staff.

But you know I'm an Eagle first. I love Coach Reid, always pull for him to do well. But in that situation I was definitely pulling for the Eagles. It was never really a thing. I'm an Eagle. It's like Kelce's mom. You have two kids in the game, you're pulling for both of them. You wish the best for both of them.

Hours after the Philadelphia Eagles blew out the quarterback-challenged San Francisco 49ers in the NFC Championship Game they learned who their opponent would be in Super Bowl LVII. The Kansas City Chiefs edged the Cincinnati Bengals, 23–20, to win the AFC championship. So on February 12, at State Farm Stadium in Glendale, Arizona, it would be the Eagles against the Chiefs. But to most people in Philadelphia it was the Eagles against Andy Reid, their coach from 1999 to 2012. The coach who took them so close so often, but couldn't finish the deal. Reid took the Eagles to five NFC Championship Games, but went 1–4 in those games. And the one Super Bowl he did get to with the Eagles, he lost to the New England Patriots.

That was the thing. And that's why some people in Philadelphia don't like Andy. He got us so close, but never won a Super Bowl. Then he goes to Kansas City and gets Patrick Mahomes and he wins the Super Bowl and wins it again and again. Yeah, I think there's some jealousy, some people are bitter. But hey, like I've said, it's a different Big Red in Kansas City than the one in Philadelphia. He's learned. He's adapted. And he's better.

Douglas had just gotten back to Philadelphia and was set to join WIP radio as its midday co-host in a major change over for the station. Except he had to wait because the station wasn't having any changes until after the Super Bowl.

Angelo (Cataldi, the WIP legend and longtime *Morning Show* host) was retiring. But he wasn't going to leave if the Eagles were in the Super Bowl. So we were all on hold. I was still doing radio in Atlanta even though I had moved back and was living in Philadelphia.

Just in time for the Super Bowl.

It was overwhelming for me. I had just gotten back to getting into the swing of being in Philly. And now to be there and to see the fan base, yeah, it was overwhelming. I had been in Atlanta for so long, almost 10 years, and in Atlanta it was more of people know who you are but it's no big deal. "Oh that's Hugh. Okay. Who gives a fuck? We know you played, but we don't care." Now back in Philly and being in that atmosphere and to be in that situation, and the Eagles are in the Super Bowl. You know Philly fans are crazy, so I had to adjust to that. It was like I was having anxiety attacks.

And that was before the game.

For the Eagles to win against the favored Chiefs they had, among other factors, to play mistake-free football and their pass rush needed to get to Mahomes. Neither happened and the Chiefs came away with a 38–35 win in one of the better Super Bowls ever played.

During the regular season, quarterback Jalen Hurts threw just six interceptions in his 15 games, although he did fumble nine times, losing seven. As far as the pass rush goes, the Eagles led the league in sacks with 70 and four of their pass rushers—Haason Reddick (16), Josh Sweat (11), Brandon Graham (11), and Javon Hargrave (11) were all in double figures.

Haason Reddick was the guy. He did so well here it's unfortunate it didn't work out. But he wanted his money.

They led the league in sacks and that was great to see. You always want to see the defensive line do well, as a defensive lineman. So it was fun to see them do what they did. And carry the team the way that they did. Jalen was still learning at that point. The defense did a really good job of making things happen. They got after (the QB) for real.

Douglas was in double figures in sacks four times in his career, but never had a teammate join him in that regard. He could appreciate what that Eagles pass rush accomplished with the pass rush coming from every angle during that 2022 season.

I never complained. You play the hand you're dealt. I didn't complain that I never played with a Hall of Famer or better players. It is what it is. We had some good players. But if you play with better guys that rush the passer it makes it easier to do what I do. Who knows how many sacks I could have had if I played with a group of guys like that. If I played with Simeon Rice, or Michel Strahan, to name a couple. Who knows? All I know is it makes everything easier.

It wasn't easy for the Eagles line that day in Arizona. Some blamed the field conditions, others credited the Chiefs offensive game plan. But that feared pass rush, the one that had 70 sacks during the season, the one that harassed New York Giants quarterback Daniel Jones in the playoffs and knocked out two 49ers quarterbacks in the NFC Championship Game, never got to Mahomes. The Kansas City quarterback dropped back 31 times, he threw the ball 27 times and ran it four times (he also took two knees), and not once did the Eagles register a sack. Not once.

Patrick Mahomes started doing Patrick Mahomes stuff. Mahomes didn't run much until the end of the game then when he had to extend plays, he did. His numbers weren't great, but he was there when it counted. He did what he had to do, what he almost always does, and won the game.

Mahomes was 21-for-27 for 182 yards with three touchdowns and ran a total of six times for 44 yards. Hurts was 27-for-38 for 304 yards and a touchdown and ran 15 times for 70 yards and three touchdowns. His one mistake, the only turnover by either team in the game, a fumble, resulted in a Chiefs touchdown.

If Jalen didn't have that fumble, the Eagles would have won the game. I truly believe that. But Jalen played his ass off. I mean he did everything. Jalen had a hell of a game. If the Eagles won he was the MVP, no question about it. But Mahomes had the big plays when he needed them and the Chiefs won.

The Eagles outgained the Chiefs, 417–340. They had the ball for 35:47 compared to Kansas City's 24:13. And they led 24–14 at halftime. Ironically what helped the Chiefs as much as anything was their running game. Reid, who seemed allergic to the run when he coached the Eagles, saw his running backs carry the ball 19 times for 110 yards. The Eagles running backs that day carried 17 times for just 45 yards.

In that first half Hurts threw a 45-yard touchdown pass to A.J. Brown and scored on touchdown runs on one and four yards. Jake Elliott's 35-yard field goal with no time on the clock gave the Eagles their 24th point of the half. The Chiefs could only counter with an 18-yard Mahomes to tight end Travis Kelce touchdown pass and Nick Bolton's 36-yard fumble recovery for a touchdown.

Brown was the Eagles big offseason acquisition. The Eagles sent the second of their two first-round picks, along with a third-round pick, to the Tennessee Titans on draft night to acquire what they felt and hoped was the missing piece in their offense.

Everyone was excited about that. A.J. was excited about it. To me he's definitely an Eagles Hall of a Fame player, but I think he's a real Hall of Fame player too. A.J. is to me the classic receiver as far as bright star, misunderstood, says controversial things, but can play his ass off. And he wants the ball. He thinks he's always open. He reminds me of T.O. a little bit.

It was a huge get for the Eagles. You know what's funny about that is that everyone was complaining that DeVonta Smith was a little too small. So they traded and got a big receiver for Jalen. And you know what makes A.J. so good is he's so physical. He's not a small receiver. He's a big-ass dude. And most of the corners he goes against he's stronger than. He just goes up and snatches the ball out of people's hands.

Brown and Smith form the best set of wide receivers in Eagles history. Brown caught 88 passes for 1,496 yards and 11 touchdowns in 2022 and followed it up with 106 catches, 1,456 yards and seven touchdowns in 2023. Smith, the Heisman Trophy winner from Alabama, caught 95 passes for 1,196 in 2022.

I think DeVonta is the better receiver in terms of he runs better routes and all of that. A.J. is just so physical. To me DeVonta is more the technician. A.J. is just a flat out beast. He's taking the ball from you. They are both very effective. It's a great combination.

Both were very good in the Super Bowl. Smith caught seven passes for 100 yards, including a 45-yard catch that set up the Eagles tying touchdown in the fourth quarter and Brown caught six for 96, including the first-half touchdown. In the second half, though, the Chiefs took over, scoring on all four of their possessions—three touchdowns and a game-winning field goal by Harrison Butker with 0:08 on the clock.

That final field goal drive, with the score tied, 35–35, was aided by a defensive holding call on Eagles cornerback James Bradberry against Chiefs wide receiver Ju Ju Smith-Schuster. On third-and-8 from the Eagles 15-yard line with 1:54 to play, Mahomes threw incomplete. But Bradberry was caught with a tug of Smith-Schuster's jersey. And the flag flew. Without the penalty, Butker would have likely still connected from 33 yards out. The Eagles, however, would have had almost two minutes and a time out to answer, instead of eight seconds and no time outs.

(The penalty) was ticky-tack. When it happened, I thought it was ticky-tack. But my opinion and I've said this is you can't leave it to the refs. You can't put it in the refs' hands.

Douglas was back on Philadelphia radio co-hosting the 10 a.m.–2 p.m. show not long after the Super Bowl loss. He had to relay that same message to distraught Eagles fans.

They felt like we got jobbed on that call. But I was like hey you can't leave it to the refs. But there was optimism in the city for the Eagles for sure. Jalen and the weapons they had, the city was still buzzing.

Me personally, I was happy for Big Red. But sad for the city. I knew how much it meant to the city and for Jalen. He was trying to come into his own and he played such a great game, not to win. But he's here and Nick Sirianni is the head coach. And Jalen wasn't Nick's pick. So you know how that normally works out.

CHAPTER 25

COMING BACK TO PHILADELPHIA

The entire conversation kind of started, "Would you ever come back to Philly."

You know me, I said, "I'll come back if you pay me." It was kind of tongue in cheek, but then as stuff started coming together it looked as if this might be a real possibility. Then it became: if that's what you really want to do you have to push it.

WIP, the main sports station in Philadelphia, was about to make major changes in its daily lineup. Angelo Cataldi, the longtime host of the station's top-rated Morning Show, *had announced his retirement. He would stay through the Eagles season—which happened to go all the way to the Super Bowl—and that would be it. Who would replace Cataldi's huge shoes was the big story in the city (outside of the Eagles Super Bowl run)? Word started to leak out that the co-hosts of the station's midday show, former NFL fullback Jon Ritchie and Joe DeCamara, were going to move from their 10:00 AM to 2:00 PM slot to the 6:00–10:00 AM* Morning Show *slot. Now, the question became who was going to fill the midday spot.*

My son, Harper, was in Philly. His mother was in Philly. So I really didn't see him that much. The opportunity to move back there presented itself. So I was like, if the opportunity is there maybe I'll pursue it. I went to my boss and gave him the reasons why I would like to go back to Philly. He was like, if you feel that strongly about it then that's fine. He said he understood what I was saying, and he didn't have a problem with it. So that's how it all started.

Now don't get me wrong, it was tough for me to leave Atlanta, because as I've said I loved it there. I love the city, the people, the listeners, it was a great time and a great experience for me. But I just thought this was a good opportunity for me to go back to Philly.

Douglas was still popular in Philadelphia as a former Eagles Pro Bowl player and now an Eagles Hall of Famer. He had worked at WIP in the past, filling in for different hosts during the week, going on with Cataldi and the Morning Show *team and also doing shows on the weekends. He had made a name for himself, and also got valuable experience the past nine years in Atlanta as he grew from doing Falcons pregame shows to being a regular co-host of the station's* Morning Show. *It was a natural fit in many ways.*

WIP agreed.

They paired Douglas with radio veteran Joe Giglio, who had been doing evenings 6:00–10:00 PM for the station.

I didn't know Joe. But you know in this business you can't keep secrets. It is what it is. We started hearing how they were going to put us together. So we followed each other on Twitter, but we never said anything to each other. We just followed each other. I'm pretty sure he was listening to me to see what I sounded like and I listened to him for the same reason.

What's funny was when we first started working together (in February 2023) it was like I knew him my whole life. You know me, I'll talk about anything on the air. I like to talk about how I like doing gummies, getting drunk, especially here, but all within reason and being responsible. I always feel like people want to feel like they know you. So I let them know me. And Joe is cool with that.

Douglas and Giglio have become a good team and are among the top rated midday shows in Philadelphia on a regular basis. The 2023 Eagles looked like a good team through the first 11 weeks of the season, and then …

It just fell apart.

Through the first 12 weeks of the regular season the Eagles laughed at the supposed "Super Bowl loser jinx" No NFC team since the 1974 Minnesota Vikings had lost a Super Bowl and returned to the Super Bowl the following year. No NFC team since the 1971 Dallas Cowboys had lost a Super Bowl and went back and won it the following season. The Eagles, off to a 10–1 start to the season, were about to change all of that.

Or at least they thought they were.

The Football gods were looking out for them early.

In those 10 wins, seven were by one score and five were by less than a touchdown. They struggled past some bad teams, such as four-win New England, 25–20, and four-win Washington, 34–31, and they got very fortunate in wins over very good teams, such as Buffalo, 37–34, and Kansas City, 21–17. In the Monday Night Football *win over the Chiefs, the Eagles won when Kansas City wide receiver Marquez Valdes-Scantling dropped what would have been the winning touchdown pass in the final minute. The Eagles only loss in those first 11 games came to a team it had never lost to before, the New York Jets. Prior to 2023, the Eagles were a perfect 12–0 against the Jets. Maybe it was an omen of what was to come.*

It all began to come unraveled in a rematch of the 2022 NFC Championship Game against the San Francisco 49ers. San Francisco dominated the Eagles in Philadelphia. And after that 42–19 loss the season was never the same.

Jalen (Hurts) looked clueless. And I think there was some dissension in the ranks. I don't think Jalen was comfortable where he was. There was just so much going on that season. And they threw the ball a lot. So then the questions started: Was Jalen the right guy for this team? There were all kinds of questions being asked. And nobody had the answers.

After Super Bowl LVII the Eagles lost more than the game to Kansas City, they lost both of their coordinators. The Indianapolis Colts hired Nick Sirianni's offensive coordinator, Shane Steichen, to be their head coach and the Arizona Cardinals hired his defensive coordinator, Jon Gannon, to be their head coach. The Eagles promoted from within to replace Steichen with quarterbacks coach Brian Johnson, who had a longtime relationship with Hurts and his family. They went outside the organization to replace Gannon with Sean Desai, who had worked with the Chicago Bears and more recently the Seattle Seahawks.

I thought it was a good look to have someone who knew Jalen personally, knew his family and everything. But I remember the Washington game, the Commodores—I know it's Commanders, but I call them "Commodores." It was late in the game and all the Eagles have to do is run the ball and put it away. The game is almost over. It's just common sense. But they're throwing the ball. And I say to myself, "What the fuck are they doing?" It was just weird.

The offense scored 433 points over the 17-game season, but was held under 20 five of the last seven games when the team went 1–6. Hurts threw 23 touchdown passes, but his interceptions rose to 15 and his quarterback rating fell to 89.1. Defensively, it was worse. The vaunted pass rush from the year before disappeared, other than Haasan Reddick, and even he went from 16 sacks to 11. Josh Sweat went from 11 to six. Brandon Graham went from 11 to three. And Javon Hargrave went from 11 to San Francisco as a free agent. The defense allowed 428 points on the season and allowed 27, or more, in five of those last seven games.

Desai was demoted and replaced by longtime Patriots and Bill Belichick assistant Matt Patricia, who was serving as a consultant, late in the season. But it just got worse as the team lost to Dallas, 33–13; Seattle, 20–17; Arizona (and Gannon), 35–31; and to the New York Giants, 27–10, to close the regular season at 11–6.

The defense was disjointed. It just didn't look right. Then they get rid of the coordinator, or demote him, whatever, and they give it to Matt Patricia. And I remember Patricia telling me, "I don't want to run somebody else's defense." But he had to run the defense. It was wild how it all happened. And it put Nick in a bad spot. It was just a real bad situation all around. It felt like he had no say on his coaching staff. It was just crazy. And then he started getting a little defensive with the questions he was being asked. It was all just crazy.

The 10 early wins, and then one more against the Giants in Week 16, were more than enough to qualify for the postseason. The Eagles grabbed the NFC's fifth-seed, or top wild-card spot. That meant a game in Tampa Bay in the first round to face the NFC South Champion Bucs, who were just 9–8 on the season and had lost to the Eagles back in September. In Tampa Bay's final two games of the season, both divisional games with the division on the line, it scored 13 points in a loss to the New Orleans Saints and nine points in a win over the Carolina Panthers. Surely, the Eagles had a chance to win this one.

It was never close.

Tampa led 13–0 before a Jake Elliott field goal made it 13–3. It was 16–3 when Hurts threw a touchdown pass to tight end Dallas Goedert and then for some reason went for a two-point conversion and failed. Tampa outscored the Eagles 16–0 in the second half on the way to a 32–9 win which might be the most embarrassing playoff loss in Eagles history.

The way it fell apart, it was kind of valid. Nobody knew what happened. It was just weird. You would talk to coach Sirianni and ask him who was calling the plays and he would get defensive about it. Like I said, it was weird. You didn't know what was going to happen next. But it was nothing good.

Then the next year comes and they right the ship.

CHAPTER 26

BIG RED VS. EAGLES II (SUPER BOWL LIX)

It started with Andy Reid. Whether you want to say it or not, that's where it all started. And all the success the Eagles are having, all the success Howie Roseman is having, it started with us. It's like your kids. You want your kids to be better than you, to have more than you. For me to see Jalen Hurts and these young men, the whole organization, the Philadelphia Eagles having the success they're having, I love it. They deserve it. And to beat the guy who started it all, that's pretty big.

For the second time in three years the Eagles met Andy Reid and the Kansas City Chiefs in the Super Bowl. After losing Super Bowl LVII in heartbreaking fashion, the Eagles left no doubt in Super Bowl LXIX with a convincing 40–22 rout of the two-time defending Super Bowl champion Chiefs.

You know how I feel about Andy. But like I've said before when they played, I'm an Eagle. I'm a Philadelphia Eagle. But I'm thinking this is going to be a squeaker, just like the last one. How many times have we seen (Kansas City quarterback) Patrick Mahomes pull a game out at the end? Keep it close and then he does his magic. But man they came out and they put hands on Patrick Mahomes. I'm not talking about healing hands. They just took it to him.

Kansas City's seven first-half possessions went punt, punt, punt, pick-six, punt, interception, punt. The Eagles led 24–0 and their defense outscored the Chiefs' offense. By the middle of the third quarter it was 34–0. Still, not every Eagles fan was relaxed.

They're up big. and I'm like, you never know, Kansas City might come back. Guys I'm with are telling me I'm crazy. But we've seen Mahomes do it before. We've seen this movie before.

This one had a different ending. Mahomes and the Chiefs scored some garbage points late, but this one was over early. The Eagles' defense dominated a poor Kansas City offensive line and the Eagles' offense took advantage of what Kansas City tried to do defensively.

(The Eagles) didn't blitz. They just let their defensive line beat up the Kansas City offensive line. And they did it all game.

On the other side, Spags (Kansas City defensive coordinator Steve Spagnuolo, a longtime Reid assistant) was resigned to let Jalen beat him with his arm. There were a few times the blitz came free off the corner and Jalen found the open receiver. He made them pay. But Spags was convinced that Jalen wasn't that dude. He kept blitzing and Jalen kept making him pay. Kansas City wanted to take Saquon (Barkley) out of the game and they did. But Jalen stepped up. Jalen was the MVP and he deserved it.

Kansas City's defense held 2,000-yard rusher Barkley to 57 yards on 25 carries. Hurts, however, ran for 72 yards and a touchdown on 11 carries and completed 17 of his 22 passes for 221 yards and two touchdowns, one each to A.J. Brown and DeVonta Smith. Mahomes threw three touchdowns, all in the final 15:34 after it was 34–0. He also threw two interceptions, one returned for a touchdown by rookie Cooper DeJean, and was sacked six times.

And for the second time in eight years the Eagles were Super Bowl champions.

This team is built to win. They have most of their guys signed for the long term now. They have a chance to go on a run, a legitimate run.

It didn't look that way at the end of 2023 when the team lost six of its last seven games and got blown out of the first round of the playoffs by Tampa Bay. Changes were made. Not the ones everyone wanted. But the ones that were needed.

Everyone questioned Hurts, the quarterback and Nick Sirianni, the head coach. The organization put it on the coordinators instead. Both Brian Johnson on offense and Sean Desai and Matt Patricia on defense were fired. They were replaced by two interesting coaches with interesting résumés, Kellen Moore and Vic Fangio.

Kellen Moore, I knew he coached the Cowboys (as quarterbacks coach and then offensive coordinator), played for the Cowboys. So for me it was the whole Dallas Cowboys thing. You looked at him reluctantly. But you do know when he was with the Cowboys they had a good, strong running attack with Ezekiel Elliott, so you do know that. Fast forward, he's here and it's the first game of the season and they're trying to throw the ball a lot. I think they were trying to figure out the offense. I was told the first couple of games it was Kellen Moore. Then Nick went back to what he knew. And it was more Nick's offense. But who knows? It took time for them to figure out what they wanted to do. When you have A.J. and DeVonta you want to be a passing team. Then you see what Saquon is doing. I think they were worried a little about over using him because he had injuries in the past. But you see how he was playing, so just lean into that.

Because nobody could stop it.

The Eagles began their Super Bowl season just 2–2 and had an ugly loss to the Atlanta Falcons on Monday Night Football. *The team blew a late lead and a dropped pass by Barkley allowed the Falcons to come back and win in the final seconds. They were also blown out in Tampa again. Then came an early bye week followed by a 10-game winning streak.*

The defense carried them early. And that was Fangio. He was a cast off from the Miami Dolphins. They didn't want him. They talked bad about him. And all he can say is, "How do you like me now?"

I liked him then. He reminded me of Jim Johnson a little bit. No nonsense, matter-of-fact kind of guy. He's old school. It was a hot day at camp and I heard him say, "Hot is a mindset. There's going to be hot days. You can't quit. You can't give up because its hot." I'm paraphrasing, but you get the point.

Football is one of the greatest brainwashing games on the planet. I firmly believe that. You're convincing a bunch of men to run through a brick wall for you. You're convincing them to do things that they normally wouldn't do. In a nutshell that's what football is. Believe in me, believe in what I'm trying to do and then go out there and do it. That's what it is. That's what Andy Reid did when he was here. And that's what Vic Fangio did. And it was impressive because what those guys said about him in Miami. Oh, he's too hard, nobody likes him. You know what he is, he's a truth teller when nobody wants to be told the truth.

When I think about the Miami Dolphins and what they said, that's why you get your ass kicked when it's cold outside because you're a bunch of pussies. You didn't have the right mentality. In football you need to be pushed and Vic Fangio pushes. He pushes you to be better.

People don't realize how rare that it is to play the way they did in one season and to have the kind of success they had in one season. It took Jim Johnson, as great as Jim Johnson was, it took us two years to get comfortable with the scheme he was running. And these cats they came in and they had a Super Bowl–caliber defense from the start.

On the personnel side the Eagles added two key players, one was the big-time signing of Barkley away from their NFC East rival the New York Giants in a move that surprised a lot of people around the league. The other was as under-the-radar signing as there was, linebacker Zach Baun, a special teams player and backup outside linebacker from New Orleans. Then there was the concept of replacing two franchise legends, center Jason Kelce and defensive tackle Fletcher Cox, who both retired after the 2023 season.

They had some young guys ready. (Defensive tackle) Jordan Davis, now he's not a pass rusher, he's a run stopper. I remember him at Georgia. I'm watching him and asking, "Why isn't he getting to the quarterback?" My friend says it's not what he does. He comes to Philly and people think he's Jerome Brown. That's not who he is. He gets a lot of heat, but to me he's the unsung hero. He does the dirty work. People don't understand that.

What's funny about Kelce is he's a Hall of Famer, no question. But when you talk about centers. Center is the one position where you have help to the left of you and to the right of you. Kelce worked to become the player that he was. But Cam Jurgens is a better athlete, with all due to respect to Kelce. I remember when people wanted to get rid of Kelce. He worked hard to become what he was. To me there was no drop off.

People said how hard it was to replace him. But he was protected by the two guards and now you have someone who is more athletic. Cam is a hell of an athlete and he's bigger.

While Kelce and Cox were not as difficult to replace as most thought, the additions of Barkley on offense and Baun on defense were huge difference makers. Barkley led the league in rushing with 2,005 yards. Baun, who was moved to inside linebacker, filled the defensive stat sheet with 150 tackles, 11 for a loss, 3½ sacks, 14 pressures, five forced fumbles, a fumble recovery, and an interception.

Zach Baun, never been a starter, was a special teams guy. He comes in and he plays lights out in that first game in Brazil against the Green Bay Packers. And he goes on to have an All Pro year. Guy came out of nowhere. Zach Baun was a special teams player, that's it. Now he comes to Philly and he's an All Pro. And got a ton of money because of it.

Barkley was another castoff from the Giants. They embarrassed him on (HBO's) *Hard Knocks*. He can't be living a better life than he is now.

I was surprised (the Eagles signed him) because running backs were dying out. They were dinosaurs. They were being phased out. The Eagles gave him some money, more than what people thought, and he resurrected that position. He made running backs relevant again. But look at defenses today. When we played we had Trot (Jeremiah Trotter) at middle linebacker. He was 250 pounds. Now the average middle linebacker is around 230. Barkley is 230. You have an equalizer now. You have a big back and the biggest offensive line in the league. So why not run the ball?

Barkley ran the ball like no Eagle had ever run the ball. Not Wilbert Montgomery, not Ricky Watters, not Brian Westbrook or LeSean McCoy, not even Hall of Famer Steve Van Buren. Barkley ran for 2,005 yards on 345 carries in 16 games. He could have challenged Eric Dickerson's NFL record of 2,105 yards set in 1984, but the team decided to give him off the final day of the season against his old team, the Giants. Barkley didn't just use his power to run over defenders. He leaped over them—sometimes in reverse. Just ask the Jacksonville Jaguars.

That Jacksonville game I was on the field. I was with Brian Dawkins and Brian Westbrook. We're having a conversation. When that play happens, I was like, "What the fuck did I just see?"

And Westbrook is, "Did you just see that?" We were all like what just happened. To be on the field and see that. Everybody was in disbelief. To be there and see it in person and be on the field. You know at that point this was going to be a special season for him and the team.

A late-season loss to Washington, in which Hurts left in the first quarter with an injury, cost the Eagles the NFC's No. 1 seed. It didn't matter. As the No. 2 seed they beat the Green Bay Packers in the first round of the playoffs, the Los Angeles Rams in a snowstorm in the divisional round and broke the 1–1 season series tie with Washington with a 55–23 rout in the NFC Championship Game.

Hurts threw for just 131 yards in the win over Green Bay and for just 128 in the win over Los Angeles. Yet he was efficient in both wins with quarterback ratings of 111.4 and 91.3 respectively. In the NFC Championship Game he completed 20 of 28 passes for 246 yards and a rating of 110.1. In the Super Bowl, he was the MVP.

Quarterback, to me, is more than just your skill set, it's leadership. And Jalen, say what you want, he does whatever it takes to win. He allows his playmakers to make plays. He'll take the back seat. But when he has to step up, he steps up big. In the Super Bowl he played his best.

Nobody believed in Jalen, that's a fact. He gets the most criticism and he rises above it. And during the course of the season nobody was happy with Jalen. Until they won. Then that changed everything.

CHAPTER 27

HUGH'S FAVORITES

One of my favorite teammates of all time was Hollis Thomas. Hollis was always with his shenanigans. But he always kept me in line, especially on the field. We would be in the huddle and I might be going off on a rant about something and I would forget the defense we just called. I would completely forget it. Mostly because I was yelling and screaming at someone. And I would be, "Oh shit, what did we just call?" And Hollis was always there to remind me what the call was. He would tell me what it was and what I was supposed to do. And then there were plays where I would go off script. I would definitely go off script a lot and Hollis was there to have my back. He was there to cover for me. So yeah, I have to say Hollis was my favorite teammate.

Here are some of Hugh's other favorites in his 10-year NFL career.

Favorite Game

It has to be the "Pickle Juice Game." First game of the season (in 2000). That's when it kind of got started. Everyone talked about how hot it was that day and Dallas tried to make a big deal of it. We beat the brakes off Dallas that day.

Opening day 2000 the Eagles, coming off a 5–11 season in Andy Reid's first year as head coach, went in and routed the Cowboys, 41–14, behind a 200-yard rushing day from Duce Staley. The Eagles would go on to finish that season 11–5 and beat Tampa Bay in the first round of the playoffs.

Before the game, Douglas laid into his teammates with a passionate speech.

Everyone was complaining about how hot it was before the game. I just told them all to shut up and just go play football. I didn't want to hear about the heat.

Favorite Plays

That's tough. One of them has to be Donovan McNabb to Freddie Mitchell against Dallas. When Donovan ran around forever and then found Freddie wide open down field.

That happened on Monday Night Football *in Dallas, during the Super Bowl season of 2004. Television timed it at 14.8 seconds that McNabb scrambled behind the line before finding Mitchell for a long gain. The Eagles won the game, 49–21, on the way to the NFC title.*

Me personally, if I had to pick one it would be the sack of Shawn King in the playoff game against Tampa Bay. That was a big play in a playoff game.

It was the Eagles' first playoff game, under Reid, and the first playoff game ever for Douglas in the wild-card game in 2000. Tampa Bay led 3–0 late in the second quarter. The Bucs faced a third-and-19 from their 25-yard line and the game changed. Douglas beat his man, sacked King, and forced a fumble. Mike Mamula recovered at the 15 and four plays later Donovan McNabb scored on a five-yard run. The Eagles took a 7–3 lead on the way to a 21–3 win.

Then the other one would be the hit on Jim Miller in the playoff game against the Bears in Chicago. That one because the Bears were just talking shit the whole game.

Favorite Opposing City/Favorite Opposing Stadium

Atlanta for both. The atmosphere in the stadium was always crazy, especially when Mike Vick was the quarterback. It was a fun place to play. And then the city because of how well they treated me when I was there.

This wasn't an easy task. Playing with so many good players in his years with the Eagles, but Hugh picked his all-time favorites by position.

Favorite Teammates

QB: Donovan McNabb—Donovan, it has to be Donovan. He got us started. He led the offense to all those playoff games. He was our leader.

RB: Duce Staley—It's close, but I have to go with Duce. But B-West (Brian Westbrook) has to be there too as a honorable mention. I remember when Duce became Duce because Charlie Garner didn't want to play. He would run one or two plays and be like, "Duce, come and get me." I'll never forget that.

And then Brian Mitchell. B-Mitch he was my man. We'll make him the returnman.

WR: Todd Pinkston—Pink is my favorite. He was my frat brother, so there's that. But Todd got a bad rap. He was fast. He could really run. He was just so thin, but he could fly. He got a bad rap for the Sean Taylor thing (in a game against Washington where he short-armed a pass where Taylor, Washington's All-Pro safety, was bearing down on him). But Pink probably still wouldn't have been right if he took that hit from Sean Taylor. It was a bad look at the time. But c'mon, Pink was probably about 170-something pounds soaking wet and Sean Taylor was putting people to sleep back then. I never blamed him for that. He would have never been right if he took that hit.

James Thrash would be my second receiver. He got a bad rap, too. They used to call him "Trash," that wasn't right. That guy worked hard.

TE: Chad Lewis—You're talking about a guy who was cut more than once and when Andy got to Philly he became a Pro Bowl player. Chad worked hard and you respect that about him, at least I did.

T: Tra Thomas and Jon Runyan—Jon brought that attitude that helped change the team. He become the catalyst for the team in that way.

Tra and I were always close. Tra came out of Florida State and was highly touted, but he put in the work. He and I did a lot of work together.

G: John Welbourn and Doug Brzezinski. Doug was a little different. Both of those guys were different. They were hard-nosed, tough guys. They weren't the most athletic, but they worked really hard. They were hard workers. That's what I remember most about both of those guys.

C: Bubba Miller—He was there when I first got to Philly. He came from (the University of) Tennessee and he was a character. When Big Red got here Bubba lost his job. But I liked Bubba. He was a good dude.

DL: Hollis Thomas, Brandon Whiting, Mike Mamula, Greg Jefferson—I used to get on Brandon's nerves. I got on a lot of guys nerves, but Brandon was cool.

Corey Simon came later and he was the best lineman I ever played with by far. The best tackle and the best lineman. He pissed me off (when he asked for his No. 53), but he was the best.

MLB: Jeremiah Trotter—Trot was No. 1 because he was a difference maker. He could change a game. They don't have linebackers like Trot around that much anymore. He was big and he could move.

OLB: Carlos Emmons and Mike Caldwell—Carlos was a good player, better than most people realized, very underrated.

Mike was a smart player. I remember a game in Arizona. Mike cramped up and was in pain and he was calling for his wife. "Sue, where's Sue. Where's my wife." I still remember that.

CB: Troy Vincent, Bobby Taylor—Have to go with Troy and Bobby and then honorable mention to Al Harris. That was a really good secondary.

S: Brian Dawkins, Tim Hauck—Everyone knows Dawk and what he did and what he brought to the team. The Mailman (Hauck), though, was that dude. He delivered.

HC: Andy Reid—Yeah, it's Andy for sure. But honorable mention to Ray Rhodes. Ray was just raw and uncut. He was so raw and uncut. You had to love him as a player who played for him.

Assistant Coaches: Leslie Frazier, Steve Spagnuolo, and John Harbaugh—Really liked all of those guys and they all went on to become head coaches.

Here are some of the toughest players Douglas had to face in his 10-year career.

Toughest Opponents

QB: Peyton Manning, Indianapolis Colts—I'll never forget that year Peyton came to The Vet and him and James Mungro went roughshod over us. Everything Peyton did it looked the same. Everything was off the same look and that made it hard for the defense. It was a hard spot to be in for sure.

RB: Stephen Davis, Washington Redskins—When I first got to Philly he was a load. That was a grown-ass man for sure. Honorable mention goes to (Pittsburgh's) Jerome Bettis.

T: Walter Jones, Seattle Seahawks—Walter was that guy. Big Walt was a wall. He was no joke. (Baltimore's) Jon Ogden was real good too.

One of Hugh's favorite people in the Eagles' organization was their public relations director, Derek Boyko. He helped him when he played, helped him get back to the Eagles after the Jacksonville debacle, and helped him start his second career in the media.

It was bittersweet. When I got here I enjoyed it. I like the city of Philadelphia. I enjoy it, I do. Sometimes the fans get on my nerves, but that's with anything. Some days are better than others. Derek was always a big help in a lot of ways.

Getting traded to Philly, though, set me up for everything, the radio, everything. Who knows what I would be doing right now. Derek was the one who definitely got me into radio. He steered me in the right direction. He set me on the path. I remember we were sitting in his office and he told me, "You would be great in the media, you should be on the radio." Then when Howard Eskin got suspended, Derek was the first one who called me and said, "You need to do that. You need to get on the radio." And here I am.

CHAPTER 28

MARK'S MEMORIES

Maybe it was me.

Derek Boyko, the Eagles longtime public relations director who has been mentioned often in this book, thinks it might have been him. As do a few other people who used to work for the team. None of them, however, were there as long as I was.

For 32 years from 1985 to 2016 I covered the Eagles as either a beat writer or a columnist for *The Trenton (N.J.) Times* and nj.com. I was also at different times the Eagles correspondent for *Sports Illustrated* and *The Sporting News*. In all of that time the team went to one Super Bowl (Super Bowl XXXIX), losing to the New England Patriots.

I retired after the 2016 season and moved to North Myrtle Beach, South Carolina. Over the next eight years the Eagles went to three Super Bowls and won two.

So yeah, it had to be me right?

Of course I'm joking, kind of. But in 32 years of covering the team I saw and did a lot. I got two trips to London, traveled to every city that had an NFL team at least once, met a lot of people who are still friends, and had a few tough decisions to make.

I say I started covering the team in 1985, because that was my first full year. I covered that 1985 Draft when the Eagles made what turned out to be the worst pick in franchise history—tackle Kevin Allen—in the first round. Allen spent more time in jail than he did with the Eagles. And then one of the best picks in franchise history when they selected quarterback Randall Cunningham in the second round. I covered minicamp, training camp (we'll get to that in a bit), and of course the preseason and regular season games.

In actuality though, I began covering the team midway through the 1984 season when my good friend Jack McCaffery left *The Trenton Times* to cover the NBA for *The Delaware County Times*. Yes, back in 1984 covering the defending NBA champion Philadelphia 76ers was a better job than covering the bad and boring Eagles.

Things certainly have changed over the years.

So after getting the Eagles beat I almost lost it in a matter of months. No, it wasn't anything I did. The team was about to move to Phoenix. Word broke late in the 1984 season that beleaguered owner Leonard Tose, who had his troubles at the blackjack tables in Atlantic City, was going to sell the team. One of the jokes that made the rounds among the Eagles writers was that after the Eagles lost a game to the Colts, 22–21, Tose thought his team won. Because he thought the Colts busted. Anyway, the new owner who Tose had agreed in part with to buy the Eagles, James Monahan, was going to move the team to the Arizona desert. The deal was all but done. Oh well, those five, or six, NFL games were nice. Now I had better brush up on my hockey knowledge.

At the last minute and on the eve of the final game of the 1984 season, a 26–10 Eagles loss to the Falcons in Atlanta, a new player emerged in the game, Norman Braman. A Miami car dealer with roots in Philadelphia, Braman bought the team with a promise to Tose that he would keep it in Philadelphia.

All right, I was still going to be a football writer . . . for the next 32 years.

That 1985 season, my first, is one I'll never forget. It was the wildest offseason, maybe ever. And again the joke was the Eagles were the most exciting and interesting team in the league, except for Sundays when they were again bad and boring.

A new owner almost always means change and there were plenty and not just the new guy from Trenton, who was still a little wide-eyed and very inexperienced. Norman Braman had his own ideas of how to run a football team and it meant getting rid of a lot of veteran players.

This was before free agency so if a player's contract was up, or he just wanted a new one, he held out of camp. Braman wanted no part of that. He decided to trade anyone who wasn't there. That included the likes of linebackers Jerry Robinson, Anthony Griggs, Reggie Wilkes, and Joel Williams. Yeah, the team traded all of its linebackers. And that wasn't all. It also traded running back Wilbert Montgomery, one of its stars from the

1980 NFC Championship team and a fan favorite. I have to brag a little bit here. The Montgomery trade—to Detroit for linebacker Garry Cobb in a rare player-for-player trade—is the first story I ever broke as a reporter.

Word was out that the Eagles were talking to the Seattle Seahawks and were going to deal Montgomery to them for linebacker Michael Jackson. When I mentioned something to then–Eagles general manager and later team president Harry Gamble, who I had gotten to know a few years earlier when his son Tom was playing baseball for The Lawrenceville School and I was covering high school sports for *The Times*, he steered me away. "If I was you I would look more to Detroit, not Seattle," Harry whispered to me.

That led me to the news that Wilbert was heading to the Lions and Cobb, who had wanted out of Detroit, was coming to the Eagles. As irony would have it, Garry Cobb and I became and still are friends and worked many radio shifts together at WIP.

So that 1985 season started with a bunch of news and ended the same way when Braman and Gamble decided to fire head coach Marion Campbell with a game to go in the season. Oh great, first year on a pro beat and I'm working on a coaching search. I would work on five more after that, but this one, like everything else in 1985, was crazy.

Braman, who lived and thrived in Miami, wanted to hire legendary Dolphins coach Don Shula's son, David. They actually offered the then 26-year-old Shula a 10-year deal. Whether it was his father, or another adviser, but he turned it down. The tide then turned to Jim Mora, who had success in the USFL with the Philadelphia Stars which made him popular among the local fan base. That deal was all but done as well. There was something in the contract that Mora didn't like and he took the New Orleans Saints head coaching position instead.

And that led to James David "Buddy" Ryan, the controversial defensive coordinator of the Chicago Bears and the 46 defense.

Like him or despise him—I was in the former—one thing was certain, the Eagles were no longer going to be boring.

Two years into the beat and I'm getting quotes and stories that were funny and outrageous. Buddy Ryan was a beat writer's dream.

When Ryan had to make his first cuts during the 1986 training camp he didn't give the usual, "This was so tough. I feel for these kids …" quotes. Ryan, asked about the first cuts, said, "These guys? My wife could have cut these guys."

And there it began. Right up until he was fired after a third straight season with a playoff loss and he told us, "I've never been fired for winning." Which he also named one of his horses—Fired For Winning.

In between we got quotes where he would refer to the owner as "the guy in France." Braman had bought a villa in France and spent his summers there. And he once questioned if Harry Gamble was, "Braman's illegitimate son," because of how quickly he moved up through the organization.

It wasn't just the head coach. Ryan put together an exciting team on and off the field. Cunningham, who *Sports Illustrated* dubbed "The Ultimate Weapon," tight end Keith Jackson, defensive stars Reggie White, Jerome Brown, Seth Joyner, Eric Allen, Andre Waters, Wes Hopkins, and more were all great on the field and in interviews. Phil Anastasia, the beat writer for *Courier Post (Camden, N.J.)* dubbed this period "the Salad Years."

In Ryan's five years as head coach, the Eagles were not just entertaining off the field, they were on Sundays now, too. They won the division in 1988, Ryan's third year, on the final day of the season in one of my most memorable days in all 32 years.

The Eagles were 9–6 as they headed to Dallas, December 18, to play the Cowboys—another great Ryan quote came a year later when he said after a last-second win over Dallas, "The Cowboys know we're going to beat them. They just don't know how." Going into that final game of 1988 the Eagles could have won and still missed the playoffs, or they could have lost and made the playoffs. Their fate was going to be decided by what happened in the New Orleans/Atlanta game (for a wild-card spot) and in the Giants/Jets game (for the NFC East title).

There was little difficulty in beating the 3–13 Cowboys, 23–7, in what turned out to be Tom Landry's last game as head coach. An aside here but long after the game ended I rode the elevator up from the locker room with Landry, just the two of us. As he got off on the ground floor (I was headed up to the press box) we both said, "Merry Christmas." Who knew that would be his last ride on that elevator?

Anyway, New Orleans came from behind to beat Atlanta on a last-second field goal, so the Eagles were in the playoffs at least as a wild-card. Then the Jets came from behind and beat the Giants on a touchdown pass from Ken O'Brien to Al Toon which made the Eagles the NFC East champs for the first time since 1980.

When the Minnesota Vikings beat the Los Angeles Rams in the wild-card game (there was just one wild-card game then and only five playoff teams) it meant the NFC East champs were headed to Chicago to face the NFC Central division champion Bears. Ryan, who was loved in Chicago when he was the team's defensive coordinator, was going back to Soldier Field. And he wasn't going quietly.

"We're not going to sneak into town," Ryan said days before the game. "We're going in with our lights on and our horns blowing."

And that's what they did. Defensive coordinator Jeff Fisher couldn't believe it, but after the team landed at O'Hare Airport, Ryan directed the bus driver to drive by Soldier Field with his lights on and the horn blowing.

That arrival was just the start of another crazy episode. It was unseasonably warm in Chicago, December 30, the night before the New Year's Eve afternoon game. I'm not a meteorologist by any stretch, but the warm weather combined with other factors led to what became known as "The Fog Bowl," or as I refer to it, "The Greatest Game I Never Saw."

Right before halftime we watched what looked like smoke about to envelop the field. It wasn't smoke. It was fog and it covered the entire stadium in the second half. It was so bad it looked as if someone painted the glass in the press box white. They actually allowed the writers onto the field for the second half. And we still couldn't see anything.

The Bears led when the fog came in and held on for a 20–12 win. The first of the Eagles three straight playoff losses. The following year was a loss to the Rams at home and the third was another loss at home this one to Washington.

There was another aspect of the "Buddy Years" and my least favorite year on the beat—the 1987 Strike Season.

It went a long way for the players to get some of what they have today. But it was awful from a fan's and writer's standpoint. Oh, in some cities it was okay. In a strong union-based city such as Philadelphia not so much. It was difficult to get to the one home replacement game the Eagles played because of unions blocking the way. It was also awful football from the Eagles. Again some players around the league crossed the line. The Eagles stayed firm. And many think that led to their success the following season. They went 0–3 in the replacement games and missed the playoffs by a game. Ryan, as only he could pull off, presented personnel people Joe Wooley and George Azar, "scab rings" at his end of the season press conference.

In the offseason before the 1990 season, Ryan's last, I had my own decision to make. I got a call one day from then-Eagles public-relations man Ron Howard, asking if I could come down to their offices. He said some people wanted to talk to me. He assured me it was a good thing, since I already wondered, "What did I do now?"

Scott Publishing, which had team magazines in a few other cities at the time, were starting a publication called *Eagles Digest* and Harry Gamble had recommended that I become the editor and basically run the operation. I met with the people from Scott, went out to dinner with them that evening, and was offered the job the next day.

I thought about it for a while. Talked to a lot of people, most of whom advised me not to take it. Still it intrigued me. Finally, after talking to my bosses at *The Times* who made it worth it for me to stay,

I politely turned down the offer. They eventually hired Dave Spadaro who turned the job into the team's website director among several other duties and was still there as of 2025. Did I make the right decision? I think I did, but I still wonder.

Rich Kotite replaced Ryan as head coach in the quickest decision in NFL history. Ryan was fired in the morning and Kotite had the job by the middle of the afternoon. It happened that fast.

Kotite and I had our moments. He screamed at me a few times for what I wrote or said, but it was never personal, it was more personnel. He just made a lot of bad decisions and the team Ryan built began to leave via free agency one by one. When he was hired by the Jets he met a friend of mine who told him he knew me. The coach laughed a bit and said, "That guy. We didn't see eye to eye, but he worked hard I'll say that." To me that was one of the best compliments I've ever received. And as irony would have it, Rich now lives about five minutes from me in North Myrtle Beach.

Ray Rhodes was almost as much fun to cover as Buddy was. He was kind of the R-rated version of Ryan. So you couldn't get all of his quotes in print for obvious reasons. Rhodes had his strengths. His drafts were good. He made good trades (getting Hugh Douglas, for instance) and he hired a good coaching staff at least at the beginning. As has already been written in this book it started to come apart for him when Jon Gruden left to become head coach of the Raiders and Dana Bible was hired as offensive coordinator.

I always say Andy Reid and I had a love/hate relationship but not so much with the love. It was more of a respect/hate relationship. Reid did one-on-one interviews with each of the beat writers during training camp every year. He once said to Derek Boyko that he enjoyed the one with me as much, if not more, than any other. And he wondered why we didn't get along better the rest of the year. The answer was simple. Control. Andy liked to control everything. And he was good at it. But I was uncontrollable. I'll never forget his initial press conference when afterwards he sat down with a few of the writers and said something to the point of "We're all in this together." We were? I didn't take that *Eagles Digest* job. There was no "We."

One of the things I've said for all 32 years of covering the team was I never cared if the Eagles won or loss. My job was to tell you *why* they won or loss. Were there certain players I wanted to see do well, sure, that's human nature. As I said at the beginning of this chapter, I made several friends over 32 years. But as far as winning or losing, that was out of my control and not on my list of things to do. I just wanted to be fair.

Andy called me at home a day or two after the 2000 Draft, the one where they selected Corey Simon in the first round. I had some contacts at Florida State and did a long feature story on Simon and how he was a good fit for the Eagles. Reid told me he read the story and really liked it. We talked a little more and before I hung up I told him I was glad he liked the story, because he might not like my next one. It was probably not the right thing to say, but I just wanted to let him know a nice phone call wasn't going to turn me into "we."

As Hugh pointed out in earlier chapters, the Big Red in Kansas City is not the same one who coached the Eagles. Not only is he different on the field, he appears to be much different off it as well, and in a good way. I think the new Andy and I would have gotten along a lot better.

This isn't going to go over well with most of the Eagles fan base, but I liked Chip Kelly. Why? He made my job easy. As easy as any coach ever. He was very intelligent and gave intelligent answers to good questions. Bad questions? He blew them off as well as the person who asked them. I liked that, because if you've ever watched or listened to any of the press conferences you know there are media people who ask questions just to hear their voice. Like Chip, I had no time for that.

Kelly gets criticized for getting rid of some good Eagles players, such as running back LeSean McCoy and wide receiver DeSean Jackson. What did the Eagles win with those players? Getting rid of them and their salary cap allowed the team to get better going forward, as it did right after Kelly was fired. And don't forget it was Kelly who drafted tackle Lane Johnson and tight end Zach Ertz, two of the heroes of the first Super Bowl win. Even Nelson Agholor, who might not have lived up to his first-round draft status, was a huge part of that Super Bowl season. Oh, and Kelly hired offensive-line coach Jeff Stoutland. That alone should change the way fans think about him.

Doug Pederson might have been the most interesting hire the team ever made. He wasn't their first choice. And he was looked at as the guy who was a bad quarterback when he was in Philly as a player. I only covered Doug for a year, his first year. And I liked him. He had that "Aw shucks, good-old boy" vibe, because that's who he was. But he's a good man.

I was long retired when the team hired Nick Sirianni, so I don't know him any better than you do. And probably less than you do since I'm miles away. Some of the writers who I keep in touch tell me I would like him. I don't know.

People I've met since I retired ask me all the time if I miss covering the team, especially since they have gotten very good. I don't. I left on my own. Unfortunately, a lot of others did not. After 32 years and a lot of changes to the way you are allowed to cover the team and the way you write about the team, it was time. For probably 30 of the 32 years it was a lot of fun. The last two not as much. Writing this book with Hugh, however, has brought back a lot of that fun.